BALTIMORE
Imprint 2

The Waves of Change

Nedra Brown

Write One -Works LLC

BALTIMORE *Imprint 2*

The Waves of Change

Write One-Works LLC
Book Writing, Author Coaching & Publishing Company
www.writenowgirl.com
writenow34@gmail.com

ISBN:
Printed in the United States of America.

Dedication

I dedicate this book to my friend Shayla Richardson. Thank you for being a kind, encouraging spirit, who has always shared your transparent accounts of womanhood with me openly. Thank you for being a genuine spirit who believes in the power of uplifting those around you! May you receive all of the blessings you deserve and desire!

Acknowledgment

I want to acknowledge my brothers, Gavis, and Marvin Brown. Thank you both for being positive resources in my and my children's lives. Thank you for being a listening ear when I need to vent, an encourager when I need encouragement, and a role model to my children. I am blessed to have you both as my siblings.

Contents

Prologue

We've all heard the familiar saying "what goes around comes around" be tossed around numerous times—leading us to believe that those who have harmed us will eventually receive the same poor, soiled intentions they have dished out amongst the undeserving. Although this has been proven true, how long is often considered too long by the harmed party? How long can one genuinely wait, pray, and prepare for the day karma comes to pay those a visit who genuinely deserve a taste of their own unadorable medicine? I have thought about this several times throughout my young existence. Specifically, when rehashing the experiences that kept me mentally stagnated and scarred wondering when and how the devil would receive his karma tides after all his unhealthy and unfriendly invasions into my life. The most uncomfortable part about waiting for people to receive their karma is that it never shows up when you're anticipating it. As soon as you give up the act of watching and waiting and you forgive and move forward, karma always has the nerve to show itself. This predictable behavior rids you of the full right to enjoy it because now you're no longer bitter and as persistent as you were initially.

I remember the days I used to wait and wait for karma to come and bite my oppressors in the ass! I often wondered if the shock of the bite or the bite itself would be the most painful component. How would it happen? And when it did finally occur, would I be satisfied? Would they all regret their wrongdoings? And if so, would the regret be heavy enough that they would become better people based on the lesson learned? This, my friends, is a pathetic act to get caught up in because it hinders you from natural growth. We want the people who harmed us to feel the burn from their poor actions. But at what cost? Should we waste away waiting for karma to rear its ugly head in the direction of our antagonist? Or should we walk away with our heads held high and trust that, in time, the universe will disperse what is required amongst the deserving? Sitting and waiting can be very mentally debilitating for the afflicted, and it serves as a reminder to those waiting, watching, and hoping that everything comes at an appointed time.

Based on these realistic components, we should always sit patiently in our anguish and wait for the universe to do what it has been known to do. We know we are responsible for paying our rent monthly; if we don't, we know the consequence is eviction. We also know that for every action, there is an equal reaction, yet we often forget that, and we sit in anticipation, waiting for our oppressors to be charged, taxed, and evicted from our lives and spaces of unhappiness. But we should remember that even the most giant devils in our lives must eventually be served eviction notices. Certain types of harm can never indeed be stripped away from our beings, no matter how hard we try, because they have become a part of us. This harm molds how we think, act, and feel. It also contributes to how we see and interpret the world around us. It serves as the premise for our conduct and morals and can also be the catalyst that molds us into reflections of the spectacle we are against.

These factors make karma a rich and triumphant experience for the oppressed because there are so many cases where we are harmed, and the harmful party is allowed to walk away unhinged and unworthy of the freedom they divulge daily. Because they have been lucky enough to escape the supremacy of the karma they so rightfully deserve based on their actions. But many must realize you can never entirely escape karma for your evil deeds. Can you stall your Karma in a manner that can lead your observations to believe that you have avoided the experience altogether? Sure! But even within doing so, karma will always spin the block and make its return, ensuring that you reap the poor seeds you have sown by choice.

CHAPTER 1

The Tides of Grief

I wanted it all to be over! Over so, I would have the privilege to move forward, stride, and forget. There are many things about those aspirations that make them unrealistic.

I wanted it all to be over! Over time, I would be privileged to move forward, grow, and forget permanently and comfortably. Many things about those aspirations cause the desire to create a space for delusions to fester. We all want to forget the sting that comes with betrayal, heartbreak, broken promises, abuse, and overall dysfunction. While we try to operate like normal humans, hoping to strip ourselves of the pain, we never asked to know. I had done the work and was currently still doing the footwork to heal from my grievous wounds. Although therapy was helping me to move forward, it was still an uncomfortable process at times. Healing is never an open-and-shut process. Although I was becoming happier in my day-to-day journey, my happiness still fled from time to time based on the many momentous events that would occur and serve as a reminder that I was not out of the dark woods just yet.

I had endured seven years of abuse, trauma, deceit, infidelity, and mental strain, so it would be unrealistic to assume that the scars from the previous plague I had endured would disappear quickly. I wanted to wake up and have it all finally be over. I needed it to be over so my mind would no longer be a prison to my past experiences. Although those experiences helped me, they also hindered me in a disheartening way. People in the behavioral science world often point out how abuse and trauma stem from a continuous cycle that is hard to sever. It's often highlighted that "the abused often become the abuser." There are many times when I have analyzed this mere fact and wondered how and why someone would want to continue a cycle that has left them harmed and uncomfortable.

What about the sting of abuse that makes the afflicted want to inflict the same harm upon another? Why does the human psyche take on uncomfortable processes and emulate them in a more elevated form than we initially know? What makes a victim of sexual abuse want to abuse another sexually? What makes a young man who has watched his mother be afflicted by physical abuse wish to beat his partner? Often, the pain and fear of these dysfunctional cycles create a window of repetition for the oppressed. It leads them down a road where they are forced to grasp onto the things that have scarred their persons—creating a cycle that is easier to model than break. I had watched this cycle become prevalent in many around me. I witnessed firsthand how dysfunction has a way of latching on to one generation after another—leaving little to no room for the afflicted to create a culture of living that is not engulfed in the violent outrage witnessed and distributed since the beginning of time.

Although I was a product of this cycle, I was determined that it would end with me, and later generations of my lineage would not know my hardships. But how does one woman achieve such an important goal? The answer is simple: She can start with her healing process, spread awareness, and learn from her past. These components were critical to severing the unfortunate chain developing for too long.

I stared at the clock, counting until my twelve-hour shift had ended. I had been working fifteen-hour days since Dr. Braxton's passing, and although it was less than the twenty-four-hour shifts, I was used to completing with him, it was overwhelming. I had experienced my first encounter with grief after the passing of my long-term client and friend, and nothing felt the same anymore. I had never lost anyone I cared about before and losing Dr. Braxton left a hole in my heart that sometimes felt heavy, foreign, and unbearable. Dr. Braxton had been one of the most resilient clients I had ever met, and I had always assumed, based on his keen ability to bounce back, that we would have much more time together. I had learned so much from him and relied on him to uplift me at times when the long work hours, endless school responsibilities, and the overall worry about achievement became too much. I relied on his words as he assured me I could do it. "I have faith in you," he'd say as I stared at my computer screen, waiting for the words to transfer from my brain down to my fingers and allow me to type out the daunting twelve-page paper required to acquire my desired GPA. Week after week, I juggled writing numerous psychology papers, formulating manuscripts, working long shifts, and being a mom to three children. The responsibility of juggling all those things was never easy, and it felt good having someone in my corner who had achieved monumental goals, assuring me that I, too, could do the same one day despite my frequent self-doubt.

With Dr. Braxton gone, things no longer felt normal. It was as if my world had been turned upside down, and all I could do was cry, think, worry, wonder, and keep going. I had read about grief and witnessed the behaviors of others who had gone through it, never considering how horrible the sting of loss was. I never thought working with Dr. Braxton in my years that one day, I would wake up, and he would be gone. I knew he would not live forever, but I always thought the day I lived in would come much later. I tried my hardest not to be selfish when thinking about his passing because I knew his suffering was over. But it is hard not to look at an event like this and feel your selfish desires are not a priority when you miss someone. I told myself that although I struggled to accept that he was gone, I would carry on and make him proud.

Dr. Braxton had given me a job during a rough time in my life after I had lost everything and had to start over with no offering except the tears in my eyes and the pain in my heart as I watched my entire world implode in a way I had not anticipated.

Because of him, I could relocate to the big house in Albemarle County, pay my tuition out of pocket, publish my books, and gain traction in pursuing my goal to become Dr. Nina White. I never thought I would gain the traction I had and not have him by my side to witness my achievements. In the weeks leading up to his passing, I noticed how his response towards me verbally was different. And it was like he was trying to tell me without telling me he would not finish with me. Although I heard it several times and took notice, I never accepted his camouflaged warnings simply because I did not want to.

His dialect would be wrapped in statements such as "I wish you the best" or "I'm rooting for you, and I know you're going to do great," which to most would seem like a regular motivational statement, but to me, they were not. Each time he responded to an inquiry about my future, he would speak to me in a way that would let me know he was still rooting for me, but he would not be present. And that is so hard to hear when you care about someone and have had them by your side every step of the way. I kept disregarding his statements because I did not want to accept a chapter where he would not be present. I could tell he was giving up, but instead of honoring that analysis, I did what I had done all those years with him, encouraging him to keep going. Later, I realized that although I had been doing my job, it was selfish of me not to honor his tiredness. Each time he responded to me in a way that appeared to be him preparing me for his departure, I disregarded it. Although I would do so in the back of my mind, I knew what would occur, but acceptance is a hard pill to swallow when you genuinely care about someone. I knew his days were limited, but I ignored the many daily observations in my direction because I was not ready to let go. Dr. Braxton had been one of the most influential beings in my life, and I did not want to accept a life stripped of that because it felt like home. Each day I arrived at his home to work, I felt like I was leaving one home to go to another.

I remember the morning of the funeral feeling extremely sick to my stomach. I usually would navigate around nausea, still able to function, telling myself it would pass, but that morning, I knew it would not. I slipped on my tan fashion nova pantsuit, with a white undershirt, and my white high-top vans, praying Dr. Braxton would not haunt me from the grave for showing up to his funeral in sneakers. My feet were swollen, so they looked like they would pop, and sneakers were the only reasonable option. So many times, while getting ready that morning, I wanted to flee from the funeral preparation and his death experience. It was like I was trapped in a bad dream, and I knew the only way to get over it was to get through it, and that is a realization that is never easy to accept.

I pulled up to the funeral home, parking in the nearest handicapped spot after noticing no available parking spots. My heart started to feel heavy as my breathing became less controlled, and my brain felt like it would fall out of my butt. Anxiety had decided to visit me, and the unannounced visit made me think I could not continue as planned. I sat in my car, taking deep breaths in and out, trying to do the breathing exercise I had learned from my therapist, hoping it would alleviate some of my anxiety and my breathing would return to homeostasis. I thought about Dr. Braxton's words the last day I saw him before his death.

I visited him in the hospital to try and feed him because he had difficulty taking in food and fluids. I remember getting him to eat several bites of chili and applesauce while I laughed at his facial expressions as he digested the horrible-looking dish. I remember him thanking me that day for dedicating my last book to him and telling me how much it meant to him. Soon after, he started telling me how great he knew I would become and talking in a way that made me uncomfortable again. At the time, I did not realize that most of my discomfort stemmed from an intuitive space in my brain. An area that identified that Dr. Braxton would not be here much longer. This space also tried to convey that his parting words of encouragement were also words of preparation. But I could not accept them because I did not want to prepare for such an experience. It was like he was telling me he had faith in me and knew what I had become, but he also needed me to know that, unfortunately, he would not be able to come along for the ride as I had planned and witness it all in real time.

I felt like God had gifted me with someone helping me to put the pieces of a million-piece puzzle together through encouragement. I was down to my last few details, and God was saying unfortunately, Dr Braxton will not be able to attend or witness this activity. And that is heartbreaking. There I sat humbled, heartbroken, and inspired, all within the same breath as I felt grief overtaking me. Sure, it was sad, uncomfortable, and unreal, but I realized it was also selfish. Dr. Braxton had given me so much knowledge, encouragement, and assistance over the years, and I needed to be thankful for that. He had been with me through many seasons of life and elevation, and God knew that the longer he was with me, I would not move to do any more than the things I had. Because so much of who I was and what I was willing to do evolved around caring for him. Drafting novels and doing school from my laptop at home while on the clock was easy. It was also easy to start businesses and operate online. But I could never honestly go the distance and grab the things I saw for myself because my loyalty lay with caring for him, and as long as he was here, that would be where the bulk of my focus went—my days had turned into mirror images as I walked into the routine of caring for everyone besides myself. Each day, I would focus on caring for my children and Dr. Braxton, telling myself that that was all that was important for now. Each day, I selflessly did that, never stopping to consider what I was missing, what more I could do regarding my dreams of becoming a great author, focusing on being a great mother to my kids, and never addressing the burnout I would frequently experience and overlook.

I was so hurt and overwhelmed by his passing that I could not see that there were many healthy components I could also grasp hold of. So many of our conversations were cultivated around black excellence and achievement because we both valued that. I did not realize that he would not want me to be sad, stagnant, or hurt from his departure. Instead, he would like me to be grateful, diligent, and successful in all the endeavors I had discussed with him. So, I decided to turn the tides of grief and create humble ripples of gratitude anytime I thought about my late friend and client. Death is and will forever be painful, but the memories of Dr. Braxton held more than enough ammunition to turn my grief into tides of grace and thankfulness for all I had acquired from knowing such a graceful spirit.

CHAPTER 2

The Narcissist I Know

Things had been up in the air for weeks, and I was starting to feel anxious and unsettled. Being a person who despises change, I am sure you can understand why some of the complex changes I was experiencing were creating feelings of disruption. I had been in hustle mode for so long and had always had a level of structure that comforted me. Especially amongst the full loads and chaotic juggling I had become accustomed to. As soon as things became unfamiliar, the familiarity of anxiety began to creep back into my space of peace and calm, and there I stood, ready to relocate back into survival mode. I was tired of feeling uncertain, but I soon realized that would always be a part of my process until I learned to have a solid faith that didn't waiver based on my circumstances. It is easy to be thankful, grateful, and obedient when God opens doors and blesses you with overflow. Things start to become a little more taxing when the surge you have received starts to shift, and you are not confident if the shift will make your routine easier or harder.

And that's where I landed after all the abrupt changes that had taken place in my life in a brief period.

I was carrying a load that consisted of starting a new business, a boatload of bills and monthly responsibilities, three children, grieving the end of a long-term friendship, losing a loved one, and dealing with Jeffrey's new stalker behaviors despite the two-year restraining order the judge had granted me. Initially, I responded to all of this with sadness and became depressed. I was tired of trying to make light of dark situations, and certain things were more challenging than others I had been managing. I had been betrayed by someone I viewed as a sister, and I was dealing with the sting of having to end that relationship despite the memories and bond we had carried for so many years. I remember trying to make things work with her after she hurt me by doing something I didn't think she could. I remember feeling torn while analyzing what I had overlooked in the previous weeks. I also remember feeling embarrassed as friends and family made it clear that despite my shock at what Raye had done, they were not shocked by her motives or moves. I felt stupid; for weeks, I had been talking about us working together, sharing how we had finished the project. All I kept getting was negative responses from my family telling me they didn't think my working with her was a good idea; the next thing I knew, the universe sent me information confirming how my family's doubt was not as displaced as I had hoped it would be. My beliefs were not as skewed as I had originally wanted to believe they were.

The phone calls where she conducted herself with an envious micro-aggressive stance that she didn't think I was able to identify. She rubbed her betrayal in my face every day, trying to trigger a hurt response that she needed because she was not in a good space internally due to her issues and the disruptions unveiling themselves in her life. I remember the calls where she would inquire about what I had going on, only to try and create a space where she could continue stabbing me after recognizing that the wound she had made was bleeding out. Why did I sit there? Talk? I offered my advice to her when I saw she was in need. Run to her aide once her troubles started occurring? Imagine working with someone to create something and have them become frustrated because although the product is finished, you are managing a life filled with ten times more responsibilities than theirs. Imagine having someone run off with a project you created together and have them remove you from that project entirely, and they take sole credit as if you never existed. Only to turn around and rub their deceit in your face, their opportunities, and have them ask you to help them again. She was inquiring if I could give her contacts for her new work position or work on other projects after she had betrayed me in such a way.

The audacity was just as thick as the betrayal, but I was starting to recognize the pattern I had analyzed among people in my life. Why did so many people want to hurt me that I called friends and family? How could so many people know my story and the pain I had lived through and still want to create more pain for me? The answer was simple: they wanted to do these things because they knew I would allow it. Hadn't I done that many times with so many people?

The truth was that I had many people in my life who had silently become inspired by me and the things I was doing, but some of those same people became inspired and soon after started misinterpreting my position. Making themselves believe that the source of their inspiration was now also their competition. When the truth was that my only competition was my former self, although it may have appeared to many that I was doing big things and handling my load well, it was sometimes daunting. The more I achieved, the more fearful I became in the process because behind the level-up stood an extensive list of responsibilities, requirements, and unaddressed trauma and doubt that had the potential to take over my approach at any time. The truth was that I never had the opportunity or the privilege of slowing down or not working hard because I was a one-woman show. Who was responsible for three little humans who were my center. My biggest fear had always been letting those little humans down because I was all they had ever known and all they ever had. I couldn't bear dropping the ball and failing them. Being a young single mom who had been disrespected, disregarded, and unprotected made me become an overprotective mother who woke up every day with the same goal. That goal was to follow my dreams and aspirations and create the best life possible for my children. I didn't understand how someone could watch my conduct and feel envious or threatened, nor did I know how my behavior could make someone want to hurt me, but it did.

I listened to my friend rant about how she had just experienced something that set her in an uncomfortable space. She started sharing how she had worked with someone on a project and watched them post it via social media without giving her the credit she earned from helping. I immediately became triggered, and the forgive-and-forget wave I rode was no longer accessible. How dare she sit and act like she hadn't done the same thing to me. How could she sit on the phone and vent to me about her experience when I was undergoing the same experience based on her shady, greedy, dishonest actions? I realized then that I needed to speak about what I felt and did. Unfortunately, she was not apologetic, nor did she take accountability for her actions. The most I got out of her during the conversation was, "I guess I could have done it a better way," all I could think was duh, you snake, but it was what it was. And what it was like at that time was heartbreaking. So that day, I got off the phone and decided to add another boundary in my life amongst yet another person who had revealed their lack of respect and value for me.

I changed my phone number and started trying to move forward despite how hurt I was then. Two weeks passed, and she began Facebook calling me after calling and finding that my number had been changed. I watched each call come back-to-back and ignored it, telling myself nothing more needed to be said after her actions and lack of accountability. I had made a habit of forgiving unforgivable acts, and I was entering a space where I started to recognize my value and the lack of value people had regarding me. You changed your number; the message said as if that had not been obvious. That's wild, she continued. The truth was she didn't think my changing my number was crazy; what she thought was crazy was that I had placed a boundary between her destructive behaviors, hindering her from continuing. Misery loves company, and I was no longer allowing people to mistreat me due to their battles with the harmful components in their lives. I had experienced many dreadful things in my life, but what I hadn't done was allow those things to be an excuse or invitation for me to mistreat others. When I struggled, I learned I needed to protect myself and my culture because people often used my shortcomings to attack me and make me feel bad. But I also learned that I needed to be protective of myself while experiencing growth because elevation will make people want to attack you, also, but in an unusual way. When your intent is clear and positive, it can be tough to understand a person with evil intent directed toward you. The saddest realization that kept occurring was coming to the rational truth that I had been okay with seeing people prosper while I struggled. Some of those people had no reciprocity towards me in the matter. Although I had earned my keep, juggled like a crazy person, and had no resources outside of myself, people were unhappy seeing me create the life I wanted, especially if they felt that life was overshadowing theirs. These harmful, hurtful components were the same behaviors that always sent me back into hermit crab mode. They led me to spend my time alone and with my children only. I had not been lucky in love or relationships, and the commonality that kept presenting itself as the main contributing factor to my unfortunate experiences was that I had never connected myself with people of value. Only people who were drawn to me for my abilities and secretly loved and hated me for them all simultaneously. I was leading them to want to undervalue and under-acknowledge me altogether. I did this by accepting poor behaviors and overlooking red flags such as shady comments, vengeful acts, and micro-aggressive behaviors that conveyed a person's lack of sincerity regarding me. This was easy for me to do most of my life because it was a dynamic that sat with me daily in most of my interactions. It's easy to mistreat yourself when mistreatment is all you have ever known. Sadly, it was harder for me to welcome love and sincerity because it was a foreign dynamic. My experiences with horrible people made me want to wake up daily and be the best person I could be. Simply because I knew firsthand the courage, responsibility, and oath of being a good human being required, and I was determined to be different from the people I had encountered.

This was a terrible realization, but I was becoming more accepting of my truths, no matter how dark, undeserving, or hurtful. The under-protected woman will always find coping mechanisms to help her feel protected, and that's what I did! I remember battling with giving myself what I deserved so many times because it always took much brainwork to grasp that I didn't deserve all the unprecedented ugliness from my peers. It often felt like sitting in a space where you have been deemed a Cinderella-like spirit, except the universe is not offering you the invitation to the ball, the handsome prince, the golden carriage, or the glass slipper. I later realized that my main offering would come in wisdom, understanding, and strength because although there is no glass slipper, there is the blessing of learning. I was learning how people can be, what makes them operate maliciously, and what that behavior can do regarding strength-building. Sure, I was tired of being strong because, most days, we all are. But I was never tired of being smart, and the universe was constantly raising my level of awareness and intuition through my poor experiences. I would later learn how to conduct myself always to walk away unharmed. I did this by no longer overextending myself in relationships, learning not to overshare, and learning to only stay in spaces where I am valued and respected. I was no longer comfortable in relationships with people who showed envy, were disrespectful, or people who felt threatened by me for being myself. Let me just say that although these behaviors positively changed my life, it was hard and lonely at times, and sometimes, the peace I had could be so peaceful that I would often misinterpret it for boredom.

I had been around so many people and for elongated periods that sometimes I fooled myself into believing it would be wrong to walk away since there was so much history. But what is history without value and respect? What is history when you're trying to evolve, and the other person wants to hold you hostage and keep you in the past? What is history if your people are looking at the new evolved you and feeling angry because they need to be able to talk down on you, see you still struggling, and watch you in their rearview, still unable to catch up with life? At the same time, they skate past you without care or extending you a genuine hand. I had always been the underdog; in the minds of many, that was all I was ever supposed to be. The historical dynamic conveyed that I was outgrowing so many people because they were unwilling to respect my new chapters in life. They were uncomfortable seeing me in certain spaces because it did not coincide with my previous image and lifestyle. I realized people around me often talked about growth, but they didn't truly have any real respect for the concept. Especially when the person on the growth scale succeeding in the matter was not them or was not whom they assumed it would or should be. This, my friends, helped me walk away from my past, history, and dysfunction and welcome my new in its entirety.

My former friend contacted me via Facebook after being smacked in the face with an unexpected curve ball. Once more, I expressed my feelings and why I was not interested in communicating with her. I listened as she disregarded the truth, her actions, and my feelings by extending one gaslit statement after another in my direction. I knew at that moment there would be no resolve. And that had been my experience with several people. The men who hurt and neglected my children were mad because they mistreated me and my kids. Now, I was in a new space that was more elevated than the previous ones I had known, and my children were thriving despite their neglectful actions. These men were not mad and acting ugly towards me because I deserved it. Still, they were angry and ugly because they were mad for miscalculating who I was, who I'd become, what life would look like for my children, and my merit in healthier spaces despite their actions. They say the ultimate revenge is your success, and I have mastered that despite my unfortunate circumstances.

Yet there I sat in disbelief, battling with adding my lifelong friend to the list of inconspicuous haters who were not as discreet as they appeared to be. But I did what needed to be done; I blocked her and all her affiliates, kept my stance, and moved forward, not letting the grief of ending things with her overpower my thoughts. I knew I had done the right thing; by doing so, I protected myself, my peace, and my heart. I had been let down so often and forgave stuff I shouldn't have. I knew that pathology was also one of my biggest afflictions, so I did what I knew I needed to, and I didn't focus on the problem but on the solution. The only way to stop people from playing in your face is to prevent people from playing in your face. I spent the next few weeks reviewing what had occurred in my mind numerous times, looking for indicators to reveal the impending betrayal. After doing that a hundred times, I realized I needed to stop. So, I took my feelings to my therapist and laid them out weekly while mentally unraveling, grieving yet another relationship that had blown up in my face. It was good to be a good person, but I understood I needed to improve myself—starting with the things and people I tolerated. Sure, you should be good to people, especially in this day and age of shitty people and shitty experiences that are at an all-time high. The value you can take with you daily is knowing that while you tried your best to love the people in your life correctly, you also loved yourself to the best of your ability.

Week after week, I vented to my therapist, about all the chaos in my life. I was silently battling depression and trying to cope with my childhood trauma, which had formed a merger with my adulthood trauma, and that was a challenging space to be in and come out of. When people looked at me, they saw this ambitious, mysterious, independent woman who didn't allow many in—never understanding that all those components had been fostered from dark places. I walked with my head high, owning my independent nature, but I was only independent because life had taught me that there was and wouldn't be anyone I could depend on outside of God and myself. So, I owned the role and allowed it to be my essential resource in the elevation window of life. Therapy helped me to identify the trauma responses I had accumulated over the years and how those responses kept me prematurely protected and progressive. There I was, making breakthroughs and growing, but then, suddenly, that progress started to feel as though it was disappearing due to the many events that kept taking place.

Dr. Braxton had passed, and I had found a new case that started rocky. After a few weeks of working and showing off my reliable nature and a month after starting, I was offered full-time hours and a raise to a higher income level than my previous salary with Dr. Braxton. This helped me keep my business rent paid and enabled me to keep working towards getting myself to the next level. I had four years of school remaining before officially becoming Dr. Nina White, and I knew that new income could help me pay my tuition out of pocket like I had been hoping to. Things were still rough for me mentally due to the grief I was experiencing and the death of Dr. Braxton, but I kept pushing myself despite my lack of internal homeostasis. What I didn't understand was how the healing process works. I had made it through so many challenging experiences and had been addressing them during therapy, leading me to believe the worst was over, but it wasn't.

I left work after working a twelve-hour shift that had left me feeling tired and depleted. I pulled to the corner of McDonald's, prepared to turn onto my street, when I noticed a familiar vehicle pull up. I wiped my eyes, feeling the supremacy of sleep deprivation taking over as I tried to understand better what and whom I was witnessing. I thought it couldn't be, as I started weighing the effects of sleep deprivation, trying to convince myself that I saw things. I had to be seeing things; there was no way my visuals were accurate. But they were, and it instantly sent me into a pit of anxiety as I viewed Jefferey sitting in the corner. He noticed me noticing him as he began to speed off treacherously, trying to escape my eyesight, but it was too late. Once again, he had managed to avoid the premise of the restraining order, riding and navigating around my neighborhood canvasing in a stalkerish manner, hoping to gain insight into my life. The life he had violated, ruined, and undervalued. It had been a year and a half, and he was still clinging to his former pathology, which consisted of violating boundaries, laws, and the little common-sense mechanisms he had accessible to him.

I started feeling flustered as my chest conveyed that I was not all right after witnessing my former oppressor violate boundaries in his narcissistic fashion. I was tired of my peace being robbed from me, and I was also tired of feeling like no matter what I did, I could never be completely rid of the devil who had made my life miserable for so long. Why was he so obsessed? So irrational? So clueless? Why was he craving insight into the life of the woman he had harmed and hindered for so many years? How did he have the audacity to inquire as if he did not know how he had violated me, my children, and our peace? Jeffrey was a predator whose sociopathic behavior knew no bounds, and I was no longer feeling the calm I had been holding onto for weeks. Some would have ruled the incident a mere coincidence, but there was no way I could. I lived in a predominately white neighborhood, and I knew no one in my community knew Jeffrey, leaving no valid reason for him to be in the vicinity other than the apparent stalking components he clung to in a reliable form.

Like clockwork, my anxiety crept back in right away, and I realized I was not over the trauma and fear, and I started drowning in my thoughts. Thoughts that were consumed with anxiety and trauma. What did he want? What was he planning to do next? Was I safe, or did I need to acquire extra protection? Once again, I was back looking over my shoulders, feeling as if I was no longer safe. Day after day, I thought about the possibility of Jeffrey violating me again and picturing the events and how the attack would occur. I only kept considering out of fear that one of us might not make it out this time, and I was determined not to be that person. I kept Tasers in multiple easy-to-obtain spaces in my home, and there was always one in my car just in case, but the sight of Jeffrey made me consider that the Taser could potentially not be enough. Several times after this sighting, I felt like getting a gun, but after each mental exploration, I would toss the thought away. I knew guns were not a great idea in a home with children. I had always feared the many accidents that could occur after hearing the stories of young children losing their lives to an accidental shooting after facing the dangers of having a gun in the home with underage children. I also knew if I had a gun and were placed in a corner due to one of Jeffery's antics, I'd be okay with using it, and that was a scary thought as well.

Every day, I would leave the house watching over my shoulder in fear of the next irrational event at the hands of a selfish, mentally ill person I knew who had no respect for rules or boundaries. I walked around waiting, and waiting, and trying to prepare as best I could for the ball of toxicity to drop. No events occurred until a few weeks later. I entered my front door, eager to kick off my shoes, shower, hop in my bed, and relax if my mind and body allowed. My phone started sending me cash app alerts, and instantly, my attention was robbed. I received three messages via the cash app from Jeff. He had been blocked on all social media platforms and didn't know my new phone number to contact me. He had utilized the cash app to start his antics, keeping my daughter at the center of his charades. He used her as his topic to reach out despite his true deadbeat nature. I was unaware that the cash app allowed messages to be sent to your contacts. All that was required was a cash amount to be sent to the contact alongside the news. Jeff sent ten dollars alongside a message, then another, and another. In the app there were thirty dollars and three fake inquiries about our daughter. The daughter the judge had informed him he could not contact or have in his presence—the daughter he had never provided for or cared for properly. The daughter he used as a social media prop to receive sympathy from strangers after he had given his false accounts of why he was not allowed to be present. I then understood that something needed to happen for Jeff to realize that he would not be allowed to violate my boundaries further.

I had been doing a lot of healing work that was hard as hell. Going to therapy, addressing the past amongst conversations with my kids, admitting that my kids needed professional assistance to heal, signing them up for therapy, and allowing a stranger into our protected bubble formulated based on the trauma, fears, and anxiety we all knew individually. After all the stress and hardship, we had undergone, it felt unfair to continue feeling raped and robbed of the peace I was trying to keep intact. My kids were getting to a better place, and I was helping us all to become happy again. Building bonds with teenagers is complex but even more complicated when you have had those bonds tarnished due to trauma and dysfunction. My children looked up to me, and they trusted me. I had let them down by having someone in our lives whose only goal was to act as a predator, preying on the innocent and ruining lives because he was angry and bitter that his former life during adolescence had been filled with so many scars. He was unwilling to face those scars, so like many who have not had the strength or privilege to face their demons, he became an immolator of his past experiences. Leading me to see firsthand how the abused often become the abuser.

We were all laughing again and having outings together that everyone enjoyed. However, our truly introverted nature allowed us to prefer being at home instead of being out and about. We were also having group discussions filled with truth. Truths that made me cry, truths that made me smile, and facts that made me understand how blessed I was in the grand scheme of unfortunate events. My children trusted me in a way that made my heart feel full despite the sadness they had known. I remember listening to them at times during our sharing sessions that were heavy and hard to say out loud, and all I could consider is that at their age, I would have never felt comfortable enough or safe enough to voice those kinds of truths to the adult figures in my life. I wept at the sound of the events that had left them hurt, abused, sad, used, and consumed with hurt in ways I never wanted them to have been acquainted with. Nonetheless, I put on my big girl panties, listened, gave advice in the areas I could, and expressed to them that we all could heal from our past life despite the sting it had left embedded in our hearts and minds. I was good at group counseling with my children, but I comprehended that certain things were too painful for me, and they needed an unbiased party to help them learn healthy ways to cope, convey, and heal. This was when I decided to reach out and get them into therapy.

I knew helping to counsel and the console was a natural gift of mine, but I also was able to recognize when I was operating in a space that was not healthy. So, I relied on what I knew from my studies and decided the best help I could give them would be to allow someone else to assist them in these matters. While I was still there offering day-to-day guidance, talks, and motherly assistance that kept their mental health-related issues in the hands of the professionals. I wish I could say I was comfortable with my choice, but at least not for a long time. There I was, studying to become a therapist and feeling inadequate because I was entrusting my children's mental health to someone, they were unfamiliar with. The ego can be tricky, treacherous, and intrusive when allowed, and based on me knowing that, I reminded myself that my thoughts regarding the choice were egotistical because although I was their mother and long-term confidant, I knew deep down, I was not the right person for the job. So, I allowed myself to feel I had failed; shortly after, I'd remind myself that I had not, and my hurt and disappointment in myself were misleading my thoughts. Thriving was our only option, and I knew I could never rise in the ways I desired unless my children came along for the ride because we had always been a synchronized team. So, I reminded myself that I was doing what was needed to break generational curses and give my kids the quality of life they deserved. A Quality that consisted of a sound mind, love, and an overall healthy environment. Doing what's best is challenging and can be much more complicated when you've seen it done in certain areas. I had come from a culture where the adults swept shit under the rug and didn't talk about the events, the feelings surrounding it, or the pain it had caused, and I was determined not to be that kind of woman. So, I navigated from a place of love and diligence, knowing that our journey would be challenging, but even in hardship, thriving is possible.

It felt unfair to be doing challenging work in so many areas. I was often tripped up by anxiety after having my boundaries violated by the number one violator in my life. I stared at the cash app messages and decided it was time to place up another border to convey to my oppressor that I was not and would not be again eligible for violation. That day, I went to the magistrate's office, presented my evidence, and got a warrant for Jeff. Weeks passed, and I had not been made aware of what had happened regarding taking the initiative, so many uneasy feelings were festering. The victim witness advocate contacted me shortly after I started worrying again and informed me that Jeff would go to trial. A few days before his trial date, I was contacted and told that I would be required to testify, and it made me feel uncomfortable. I didn't want to have to look at Jeff, and it disgusted me every time I considered the task. I was informed that Jeff had been offered a plea, and due to his decline, I would be responsible for sharing the account of the violated restraining order. I dreaded the encounter for days while trying to prepare myself for the daunting task ahead mentally.

What I couldn't wrap my head around was how someone could claim to be not guilty and decline a plea deal when there was a substantial amount of evidence, I had that I could present in court showing the consistent violation. The text messages saved voicemails, inbox messages, and cash app attempts. The thing about people like Jeff is that they never take accountability for their poor actions. It is always easier to deny than take ownership, which has been his pathology since day one. I never bothered him, his family, or anyone affiliated with him. Nor did I make it an issue that he was a deadbeat father. So, I couldn't understand why leaving me alone was such a complex concept for him. I was tired of trying to make sense of the senseless, and I was also tired of having negative hate-filled entities desire to be in my presence when the reality was, they were filled with a level of envy and hatred towards me that I did not deserve or want. I felt like I had finally learned to swim in a pool of dysfunction, trauma, pain, and past failures. The catalyst for most of my negative memories and emotions had apprehended my growth and was now holding me underwater, trying to prevent me from continuing. Despite the negative thoughts and anxiety, I had become perplexed with due to my past, I held my head high. I prepared for court because I knew I needed to get Jeff to understand that I would not allow him to penetrate his way back into my or my children's lives.

One dynamic that had always been real was that God knew my heart, my intent, and my struggles. And like a trustworthy caregiver, he always showed up for me when I needed him the most. The weekend before the court hearing, the victim witness advocate contacted me, letting me know Jeff had decided to take the plea, and I was no longer responsible for testifying. She informed me that he would be due to report to the jail at the end of the week. At that moment, I felt instant relief as I reminded myself that no matter how hard it got or how alone I thought I was, a higher power would always support me; that was all I needed then. Although time had passed, not much had changed with Jeff's behavior. That component served as a reminder that he would always choose the lack of accountability over acknowledging his wrongs and clinging to the negative yet predictable unhealthy behaviors that were not helping his agenda as much as he assumed. Leaving him to be remembered as just another narcissist I once knew!

CHAPTER 3

The Wheel of Positivity

T hings were changing for me far faster than I was used to. It felt like I had been behind the wheel for years, working hard while trying to reach a destination internally that always proved to be unreachable. The harder I worked to try and restructure the harmful components in my life, the harder I felt that, at times, I would have to work to get myself to a space of prominence. There were days when I felt like my vision of life was assessable and others when I questioned my competence. Did I want too much? Was I working too hard? And would I be able to keep up my momentum and juggle the load constantly evolving before my restless eyes?

Although I felt like a ridiculous woman, I knew I was not. Sure, the road to my destination would be filled with chaos, responsibility, loss of hours of sleep, and hardship, but that was a price I was willing to pay. I was crazy, crazy for working long hours, but those hours brought me the capital I needed to take care of my family and go after my aspirations, which all had high financial obligations. I was crazy about juggling motherhood, work, school, business, and authorship. But all those things gave me purpose, helped me to transfer my light into the space of others in desperate need of it, and helped me to give my children a chance to see how much I truly valued them. Every day, they witnessed the lengths I was willing to explore, no matter how tired, drained, or unprepared I was. I also aspired to show them they could be limitless by modeling that behavior daily. Most of my doubt stemmed from never being told I could do certain things. I remember being chastised and having others describe what I couldn't do more than I was encouraged. This led me to understand the importance of encouragement, modeling positive behaviors, and showing your seeds that they could reach the unreachable.

I was crazy for working those long hours and then clocking out, logging into a computer, and studying long hours to get a piece of paper that would allow me to move forward and do the same for two more pieces required to become Dr. Nina White. I was also crazy about paying the tuition for that paper, knowing I had many financial responsibilities and didn't need to add more. But what do you do when you feel your gift roaring inside, waiting to be utilized? What do you do when your friends who have paid therapists call you Because they rely on your unregulated, unlicensed ear and opinions?

I had become accustomed to people calling me with their problems and having me act as a psychologist long before stepping head-first into the endeavor. The act made me feel driven to listen, respond, help, and care, even when I didn't always have room to do so. My scientific brain would kick in immediately while I sat on the other end, listening to people convey to me what negative experiences they were facing, the behaviors of the people around them, and unconsciously, the behaviors that have caused the social catalyst they seem to be facing in real-time. Instead of walking away and focusing on my full plate, I often felt propelled in the direction of the event, leading me to start conducting myself as the scientist I didn't have the time to be.

Automatically, my mind would listen, pull apart the dilemma, and dive deeper into the person's psyche to observe what was openly offered to me and what was not. I would immediately consider the behaviors and wonder why the person's conduct was what it was. At times, the conversations would be so loaded with the past and the present that I would have the privilege of pulling apart the past events that, in most cases, led to the current event and the current behaviors being overlooked. I could sense the lies, truths, traumas, and uncertainties in the person's voice, whether they chose to disclose them to me. These situations conveyed that the crazy I dove into regularly while trying to get closer and closer to obtaining a Ph.D. was more of a requirement and calling. It felt unbelievable at times, but it was what was needed to be grasped for me to do what was required to meet the needs of the people I wanted to serve. Having goals and aspirations in life is essential, but those goals and aspirations should always offer a service component you feel only you can distribute. What is the point of having accolades if you are not changing the lives of others in the process?

My children didn't always appreciate my doings, but they always recognized it. They each had moments where they would witness someone else's hardships, which made them understand how lucky they were. Having them tell me randomly how much they appreciated me always warmed my heart, making the hard days more manageable. Juggling wasn't easy, and most days, I did feel like a crazy woman, but I was a crazy woman on a mission to give her kids the best life possible. So, I think the crazy I had welcomed into my daily life was well warranted. But it still was a daunting lifestyle because there was always the fear of it all not being enough. When you're a mom, you always fear waking up one day and realizing your best wasn't enough. No matter how hard you try, you can never control the uncontrollable factors life offers us against our will. I knew the level of perfection I silently dreamed of did not exist, but I also knew that giving motherhood and life my all was a part of who I was. It was also my redeeming quality at times because it kept me grounded, focused, and determined in ways that are hard to stay disciplined in. On some of my roughest days, I would take a silent look at my children and feel thankful for their Presence because I know how they all have saved my life and made me a better woman. Some days, I look at them and say a silent thank you because I knew I could never have become the Nina White I am today without them. They have been and continue to be the purpose that keeps my wheels spinning even when I don't know how, when, or if I can continue. But I know the main reason I have been able to continue through it all is the three faces God has blessed me with the ability to wake up to every morning.

One thing I have always been grateful for is the strength God has always granted me throughout my motherhood journey. Being a young mom on my own was never easy, and I'm thankful God always kept my children as my center and kept me focused on them no matter what trials came my way. Looking over my life, I often reflect on my most challenging days because I see how those days shaped me to be progressive. I never blamed people for my shortcomings, even when their behaviors proved they were liable for some of my poor experiences. I also never stood still in a flawed moment because my experiences showed me that the only way through was through and always required a level of self-sufficiency that only comes with trial and error. Although I could never be certain which side of the spectrum of life I would end up on after facing my fears and shortcomings, I was always humble enough to know that no matter where I landed, it was all a part of my process. That ideology kept me grounded and faithful that everything was and would work out for the betterment of who I was becoming.

The hard days had ended, and I was finally walking in the portion of my purpose that kept me smiling, mindful, and calm while living a level of peace I had not known for a long time. It was as if the worst days of my existence were no longer glued to my essence in the ways they previously were. I no longer felt crippled when going out amongst familiar faces who knew my story, thrived off my pain and misfortune, or the people who flourished in the opportunity to bring up the past. The worst thing you can do when in the presence of a hater is to show them that you are no longer bothered. And that's where I landed.

People would often inquire about my previous experiences, and I would enjoy the sting of shock my lackluster response gave them once they realized I was no longer drowning in the tides of the past. My responses were filled with the wisdom, peace, and prosperity I had come to know shortly after owning my experiences and deciding that those experiences did not have ownership over me. It surprised me that the shade, subliminal occurrences, and random questioning stopped once this occurred. People are often more predictable than they will admit to. Soon after, most people who had made it their duty to be generously ugly, micro-aggressive, and pessimistic in my direction started reaching out to me with different behavior—asking me questions from time to time, trying to portray themselves as positive citizens who wanted to know how I was doing. Some of them would complement my weight loss, congratulate me on my new business moves, or simply convey that they saw the glow of peace and happiness I was now welcoming into my space. I was no stranger to fake vibes. I was also no stranger to misinterpretations, and it was clear people were starting to realize they were wrong regarding me. They were also starting to understand the determination and favor I had stamped upon my being. It no longer mattered to me what anyone was saying or doing because I knew none of it could hinder me. I also knew that God had allowed me to no longer focus on the negativity always directed toward me from others. I now knew who I was and who he was building me to be.

Based on that understanding and newfound awareness, I could cling to the wheel of positivity no matter what occurred in my space. This cognitive process was also starting to rub off on others, and people finally realized I didn't deserve the negative energy they sent in my direction. You know what they say, "If you can't beat them, join them." I wasn't fond of fake interaction, watchful eyes, or the people who loved and simultaneously hated me. However, a few decided they no longer wanted to be in a negative space regarding me, and I respected their behavior changes. I was not interested in forming bonds with those people, but I was humble enough to smile, speak, and convey that the past was the past. I would not hold grudges or anyone's poor judgments or behaviors against them. I had made many strides, but the main stride I wanted to continue formulating an ongoing relationship with was the stride that came with my bond with the ideology of forgiveness. The way I was starting to look at life was based on the main fact that we are all human, and no one is perfect. The healing that enters your heart when you forgive people is a blessing that cannot be described. Without reason, I could not be responsible for anyone's hatred or anger propelled into my space. But what I could do was allow myself to let go, forgive, and live in a space where I didn't question or obsess over people's mal behaviors. I finally understood the value of living in a space where other people don't hold precedence over your thoughts and behaviors, and that was a level of freedom I knew I deserved. The wheel of positivity had entered my realm and laid down permanent roots in my healing journey.

CHAPTER 4

To Be or Not To Be

Self-care had been something I had seen and heard many rave about from time to time, causing me to feel left out after acknowledging that I didn't have much space in my daily life for such a routine. Who has time for self-care pauses in a world where you are responsible for work, running a business, parenting, school, and so on? Although I previously thought that was an adequate thought process, it didn't take long to realize it was not. I wanted to be self-indulgent in the ways that some people were. I allowed myself the mental and spiritual freedom of a daily cleanse to help release the frustrations that manifest internally when balancing a large load, but I could not.

Sadly enough, every time I tried considering the matter, I felt like it was frivolous. In my mind, there was never enough time in the day, and I had too much shit to do! This, my friends, is a poor mindset and essentially the catalyst for burnout. What was it about my Capricorn being that would not allow me to be patient and kind to myself? Why did the thought of slowing down and allowing myself time to catch up scare me? Fear! Plain and simple! An enormous amount of fear dwelling inside of my being rent-free made me question and worry when those two behaviors were not warranted. The fear of missing my mark, losing traction, and not getting where I needed to be terrified me. I homed in on this fear so much because I had allowed so many poor relationships to hinder who I was and what I achieved that I felt staying busy and focused kept me safe. Safe from the weirdos who admired my energy but didn't want to form genuine bonds with me because of it.

Safe from the watchful eyes, which were obsessed with my every move, not because they were happy for me but because they were praying for the day I gave up, lost traction, and stopped manifesting the abundance they were all so tired of seeing. I knew there were certain people who had a dire need to see me fail because they never saw it for me from the start. But there is beauty in self-awareness, understanding your process, and having God's favor. I was also starting to be awarded the privilege of meeting other Black women who shared my experience. Hearing other people's stories about their manifestation journey helped me to understand that it was all okay.

It's hard to be okay with the negativity you didn't ask for and nosey inquiries from people pretending to be happy for you. Although you can detect the frustration, they think they are masking with fake love and fake support. It's also hard to be okay with people who have always hated you for your essence. Feeling silently triggered by your growth and development because, in their minds, you were the seed that was never adequately watered, yet somehow you managed to thrive amongst their poor judgments and misinterpretations. I was aware of the misconceptions being stamped on my being, but I also knew why certain people wanted to hold onto specific biases regarding me. I learned how much people hate to be wrong, and growing up in a manner that makes people pay attention despite what they thought they knew can be frustrating as hell for some. Growth can also be triggering because humans are naturally comparative. So, instead of observing and respecting an unanticipated transformation, they will hate, pretend they don't see what's unfolding, and spread lies about who you are.

In most cases, it's easier to create a false narrative about who a person is than to accept their truth when it isn't one you feel is agreeable to what you have previously assumed out of hate and ignorance. I had always wanted to be freed from these experiences. Hence, naturally, I overlooked the hidden blessings beneath the opposing encrusted surface of community stigmas, racism, sexism, statistics, envy, and suppression. Because, like most, I had become tired, and all I wanted was a safety net that never was accessible to me. Ironically, once I started unpacking my emotions, understanding myself in-depth, and owning my essence, none of the previous mal behaviors mattered anymore because now they made sense.

I had always been the girl who wasn't afraid to march to the beat of her own drum. Doing whatever my heart told me was right even when the people around me disagreed with my path. Homing in on who I had become made me more conscious of why the experiences I wanted to be freed from were vital for my process. Sure, there were many experiences that I felt I could have done without, but who would I be without most of my occurrences? I started recognizing that the bulk of my self-care needs were regarding protecting my mind from the under-welcomed energy that comes with overthinking, placing boundaries so specific energies could no longer have access to me, and honing in on the intuitive nature that always allowed me to see more than I wanted to, pick up on energies I barely had any familiarity with, and the trusted scientific curiosity that made me want to dissect peoples odd but predictable behaviors.

It's a blessing to wake up one day and realize that none of the above truly matters outside the standard developmental components. I understood that my process was my process, and I was in control of my now. I also recognized that I could shield certain vibes from my space. I also recognized that it was okay to be myself and take up space in a world that normalizes the suppression of Black women. It was okay to be transparent. Using my voice and speaking the truths people tried to deny was okay. It was also okay to outgrow people who did not respect who I was as a whole. Because naturally, the people we start with have a tough time accepting changes when the difference is one, they cannot become accustomed to due to familiarity.

The funny thing is that once I became aware of myself and okay with all components of my being, none of the previous details mattered in the same way. Because now, I am honored to walk into rooms showing up as me. The girl, who at first glance appeared quiet until she opened her mouth, and her words were just as alluring and noticeable as her attire. I also honored showing up as the girl who overcame statistically inspired stigmas because my teen mom status had, in turn, molded my excellence because the human life I created out of misguided intent had, in turn, guided me to a path of purpose and helped me recognize that I could achieve despite being told otherwise.

I had become accustomed to muting myself in all spaces because I thought it kept me safe and insignificant to the environment. I later learned that there were specific components of identity that could never be muted. No matter how silent or watered down we aspire to become, certain auras permeate their way through against our will—making the light we wish to conceal present and recognizable. This allowed me to understand how important it was to be my authentic self. Despite the immense hate energy, I acquired Because of it, I realized playing it safe was foolish because even when you try to tuck in who you are, who you are is still interpretable. Based on that universal law, I decided fuck it.... Show up and show out! It is better to be hated when walking towards your purpose than to be liked for holding back the goodness that is you! How can I judge the environments that oppress me if I consciously suppress myself in hopes of being deemed agreeable? Based on my findings after probing through my significant array of dishonorable experiences, I decided walking in my truth was the only way to be safe. The question of my existence was no longer based on whether I should be, or I shouldn't. Because I realized what was implanted in my being was not only for my benefit, and my purpose was co-dependent on my ability to live out loud in a way I could no longer suppress despite my former desire to be invisible.

CHAPTER 5

Transitions and Tranquility

My life had been in transition mode for months, and I faced many new challenges head-on. Although there were numerous times I wanted to flee from this new path, I couldn't help but take notice of all the possibilities I could work my way towards if and only if I did not give up. The future holds so many new and unknown promises for each of us, but there are always times when we view the possibilities with a tired lens. A lens that is foggy and unfaithful due to the many battles we've faced and won, faced, and lost, or just faced in general. I had never walked into a new space and not had to face adversity, so the concept was not foreign to me, but a part of me was tired of that sort of experience. I often wondered why God thought I could handle so many challenges and why he never cleared my slate and allowed me a different experience. Nonetheless, I knew better than to question God, his direction, and his timing. So, I did what needed to be done, sucked up my ego, discouraged my feelings of pride, and followed the path he was setting up for me. Shortly after ridding myself of the complaints and negative emotions, I realized I was responsible for my reality. The subconscious mind is one of the main resources that help us formulate a life beyond what can be seen by the naked eye. We blame the universe, God, friends, and family daily for our mishaps and misfortunes. Although this is a commonality, we never consider the role we truly play in formulating our reality.

Although we can envision the life we dream of, filled with abundance and vivacious prospects waiting in the distance, ready to escort us into the realm of success, we never truly consider how limitless we are. French philosopher Rene Descartes believed that a man is as he thinks. Introducing the world to the infamous quote, "I think; therefore I am." *Descartes, René, 1596-1650. (1986). Discourse on method.* The more intuitive I became regarding my process, the more I deeply understood what this phrase conveyed regarding the law of attraction. Most of us have been taught that if we truly desire something wholeheartedly, we should pray and ask God to send us our desire. We often start by clenching our hands together, falling to our knees, and uttering the words silently, asking for what we feel we deserve. Although this method has been proven successful, most of us never undress this action because it has been instilled in us as the most effective way to draw our desires nearby.

Descartes's philosophy was considered to offer proof of existence. If I think, then I am, which translates to man's ability to think, proving that he is real live matter in real time. This opens our eyes to the mere fact that we create our reality based on the thought processes we encompass. If I think I am a good person then I will conduct myself as so therefore welcoming that into my reality. If I believe I am a writer, a Doctor, or a pastor I will think it, then in turn I shall become those very things I feel in my heart are true of my existence. Each of those realms require accolades that often take time but nonetheless one could argue that prior to obtaining those goals one could consider the fact that "they are the person they are working towards becoming" due to the ideology of believing before achieving. Although we understand that we exist, we must also understand what each existence encompasses. Many of us do this by focusing on the purpose or point of origin for which we believe that purpose will originate and show itself to us. We equate our existence and its importance with worldly objects, social rankings, and the manifestations of our deepest dreams and desires. We have seen how prayer acts as a catalyst assisting us on our journey, but most of us don't truly understand the notion and why it is successful. The act of prayer is built upon the ideology that we are utilizing the act of faith to move us closer to the things we desire. By leaning on this faith, we convey that our worship, communication, and ability to depend on a higher source will move us closer to what we want.

"As a man thinketh in his heart, so he is" (Proverbs 23:7 KJV). This scripture serves as a reminder that what we believe in our hearts will come to be in our minds and our reality. My new career path was starting to feel overwhelming most days. I would start my day by working as an insurance agent, spend my evening cleaning my home, packing lunches, counseling my teenagers through their fluctuating emotions, and preparing myself for the long twelve-hour nights of putting in the work to build my home care business to where I wanted it to be. I had been manifesting numerous things at once, and my vision was so fixated on the things I was checking off my list that I didn't stop to think about how some of my manifestations could clash. I had worked hard to get my license and become an agent, and I had manifested the goal after becoming inspired by my two younger brothers. Both had lucrative, sustainable careers in the insurance industry working as adjusters. I saw their level of increase and wanted to follow, feeling as though it would be a smart move because I had been successfully self-employed for eight years but was tired of my success and stability being contingent upon the life of another. My line of work was fulfilling to me in many ways, but it lacked longevity because when a client passed, it left me financially vulnerable, and I was tired of having those periods in my life.

Although I was not giving up my former career path and still working on building my home care business, I started making choices that I felt were more beneficial to my overall process. I worked long days sitting at a computer in my room as an insurance agent for one of the top insurance companies in the industry as a work-from-home agent. The position was filled with challenges, and despite my discomfort, I told myself I would continue to learn, ask questions, and speak up when I needed to so I could keep building toward my goal of becoming an adjuster. I would work my insurance job Monday through Friday, during the day, utilize the few hours I had in between jobs to clean my house, pack lunches, bathe my youngest, do laundry, and get everyone organized and prepared for the next day. After completing my task, I would have time to shower and get to my overnight supervisor job, work ten hours overnight, go home in the morning, prepare for my insurance shift, and do this day in and day out. My income was good, but I was starting to view life differently, especially after realizing I desired less to be in my bag and more so to be in my bed after feeling extremely burned out, which was an on-again-off-again situation. After being a serial worrier for years, I realized that worrying about things was a major disservice. God had never let me go without, and at the right moment, he always sent me deliverance and helped me achieve any goals I set. This understanding helped me to realize that I didn't need to chase after my goals and dreams because when the timing was right, everything I desired would find its way to me. This mindset I was developing was of a more chilled vibration, and it was helping me to listen to my body and mind and make sound choices that weren't formulated around any goal or desire for abundance. After weeks of battling with what was best for me, I decided that working the ten-hour shifts at night no longer made sense, and I abruptly quit my supervisor position. Although the pay was good, I realized it was a physically taxing position, hindering me from adequate sleep and other responsibilities. I rested for two weeks, then went to work at a facility overnight, and it turned out to be a better fit. The job was easy; I could finish my schoolwork and write at night, and there were opportunities for overtime every week. Although I was back to my norm with working a lot, I still had time to sleep, and the work felt more rewarding than my previous supervisor role.

The business had slowed tremendously, and I knew I needed to continue despite the influx.

I had reached out to the same facility months earlier, and after speaking with them and having them decline the pay that I desired, I decided not to try and move forward with employment. After leaving my supervisor role, I contacted the same facility and had them agree to that amount during our first conversation. Like that, I manifested my desired pay without any kickback from the same representative who had originally declined. Shortly after becoming accustomed to my new work environment and falling in love with my job and ability to pick up overtime, I started having doubts about my insurance position. There, I sat at a desk daily, answering calls and emails and attending meetings while bored and frustrated. I could no longer do much about my business goals, and my marketing efforts had been reduced to only being committed on the weekends when I had the proper time to give to the task. I was now doing the very thing I had always vowed not to do, which was becoming a slave to corporate America. Every day, I would log in for my work-from-home shift, trying to tough it out, and although I started making progress in my tedious role, I felt a desire tugging at me daily, telling me to hang it up. There was always a persistent feeling informing me that I was no longer on my path. Although I felt it, I kept ignoring it because, like most people, I was hardheaded, and I felt I had put in too much work getting my insurance license and obtaining the career position I was currently in. I no longer honored God's will for myself because I had my mind set on many things, not understanding that some were not for me. Weeks passed, and I continued to stick it out with my insurance position, making it to my seventh month of employment with the company. Although I was starting to set my sights on long-term goals with the company, I knew the position was holding me back from other goals I had previously set for myself that were more important to me. I kept dancing around, leaving my insurance position. Still, I knew it was hindering my family, school, and business goals, and week after week, I saw my visions slipping away into an abyss of discomfort as I clung to a goal I knew did not fit well with my lifestyle or long-term goals.

One morning, I woke up anxious and excited about my plan to use my paid time off to volunteer in my youngest daughter's classroom for the morning. I had just released my first children's book, which I had co-written with one of my brothers, and I was eager to share the story with my daughter's class. I went in and read the class the story that morning. I enjoyed seeing the look of interest they all had plastered on their faces as they watched me enter the classroom, drenched in my normal esthetic of flair and fashion as I walked through the door, listening as a few students inquired about who I was. At the same time, my daughter Amaya announced to the class that I was indeed her mother. I enjoyed my morning with the class, and as I hopped into my car, I felt discontent when I thought about returning to my corporate duties for the day. The disdain that rested in the pit of my stomach was conveying to me that today was indeed the day to make a choice. After having a morning that was not filled with constrictions or restraints, the choice I needed to make was becoming easier. Having a morning where I could rip and run and not be mandated to a computer and headset felt beyond amazing after the hard workdays I had been having. Stopping by my business, checking the voicemail, and updating my calendar also felt good. Although this task may have seemed minuscule, it had been neglected week after week due to my tedious work schedule. I was starting to understand the importance of a work-life balance, and it was becoming clearer that there was no balance in my daily realm. So, I leaped and said Fuck it! I quit! The irony is that I chose to do this a day after I had just had a salary increase and a positive meeting with my supervisor about my career goals and options to help get me to where I needed to be. I should've been concerned about the benefits and income, according to most. Everyone I informed about my choice thought I was crazy for making such an abrupt decision, but I knew it would work out. That was simply because, looking back over my life, I couldn't analyze one single isolated event where it hadn't worked out in my favor, and based on that, I walked into the next chapter of my life with peace and faith that the choice I made would put me back on the right path, and sure enough it did and fast!

Seventy-two hours after making this choice, I had not one but two new clients, a new schedule that allowed me to have the time I desired with my family, and my income doubled. I told myself this progress had occurred based on my ability to trust the process, listen, and obey what God was revealing to me despite my discomfort regarding the matter, and most importantly, that increase had been delivered fast based on my ability to have confidence in myself. Things started picking up within a week, and I was back on the road to being a full-time caregiver like I had always done. I would get up every morning and have a healthy breakfast, meditate, write, and do one productive act a day before falling into a coma and sleeping until it was time for my youngest daughter to arrive home from school. I was still on a schedule, but it made more sense in terms of my goals, my responsibilities, and, most importantly, my body's need for an adequate amount of rest. Just like that, I was walking into a new space that kept me filled with gratitude and abundance. I thank the universe daily for my overnight position that I was falling increasingly in love with, my new clients who were not stressful, and the financial status that was three times more than what I previously earned as an insurance agent. My clients and my night position all allowed me the privilege of getting my schoolwork and writing completed. Instantly, I was back on the road to pursuing my goal of obtaining my Ph.D. and producing the many manuscripts that roamed in my head throughout the day. I could still stay on top of the millions of piles of laundry that never seemed to depreciate truly, my home was still organized in the way I preferred, and my mothering responsibilities were all completed to my liking. I was shocked at how quickly things had improved after I chose. I felt like God was conveying to me that, like always, he was still on my side and leading me down the path that would allow me to manifest all the things I saw for myself, but his doing so would require me to elevate to a higher level of faith than what I had previously.

CHAPTER 6

Imposter Syndrome

T hings were constantly transitioning, and I felt overwhelmed by my ability to keep up with all the changes simultaneously. I had finally encompassed a more passive behavior regarding the seeds I was sowing, and at times, it felt odd. There I sat, watering my seeds daily without the constant flush of anxiety that had originally caused me to hover over every seed I planted, waiting for the vision to transition from my imagination into reality. I realized that Einstein was truly on to something when he said, "Imagination is everything; it is the preview of life's coming attractions." I had started to understand how everything I had envisioned was manifesting into my reality, leading me to understand why hovering was unnecessary. I started to see how everything that was once a mere imaginative idea became a part of my reality based on the footwork I had been doing daily.

I started to understand that there was no need to be anxious or worrisome about the future Because I had been creating the future daily for quite some time, and everything was starting to flourish in the ways I needed it to. I had started my home health agency, and after having periods of ups and downs and watching it constantly fluctuate to and from its six-figure status, I finally started seeing the kind of consistency I needed, and that was a feeling I couldn't begin to describe. I remember the many moments of frustration when I started to feel anxious about the future of my business after seeing it tinker up and down. Although I knew that was a part of any new business, especially a home health business, I couldn't help but feel frustration as I dished out money monthly for a business that was not as stable as I had preferred. Despite my constant struggles, I decided to do things differently this time regarding business. In the past, when I experienced these predictable yet uncomfortable moments, I would drop the ball and give up all together. Still, this time, I promised myself I would see things through even when I felt the sting of adversity riding my coattails. And I kept my word, dishing out money every month, creating marketing material, canvassing in the city and surrounding counties, and most importantly, I prayed. Every day, I would start my morning off by consuming my mind with positive affirmations, meditation, and prayer, and just like clockwork, I was fortunate enough to witness how prayer changes things. After an elongated period of first-year ups and downs, my business started thriving consistently. I was starting to see my vision flourishing in the ways I had hoped, and it was almost unbelievable at times. I remember the day I got the call that set things back in motion for me. All I could think about was how I kept saying I felt like things were about to turn around, only to be able to acknowledge that things indeed had turned around. I enjoyed life in ways I had always hoped but never truly imagined. After my business started to pick back up, I found myself at a crossroads Because, like usual, life had hit me with a flow of abundance that came all at once. Like always, there was a list of hard choices I had to make to flourish and keep up with the traction of life positively and stably. I had previously been working for an assisted living facility, and my original goal was to do so until my business returned to its former status. Still, unfortunately, I had fallen in love with the job and knew I would not be willing to drop the position altogether. I loved the residence; I could pick up as little or as many hours as I preferred. The overtime option allowed me to bring home what I would if I worked a monthly private case. This was a blessing because this allowed me to keep up with my financial obligations and have the stability that home healthcare jobs do not offer. I decided that although my business was booming again, I would keep my position at the assistant living facility for at least four more years while I pursued my degrees. This would give me the stability I needed without having to experience financial instability. This also made it easier for me to enjoy the fruits of my labor due to my business income being an additional source that, at times, I did not have to utilize.But would I did not anticipate was the level of growth and abundance God would send me that would place my business at a level of growth that would require me to focus only on that and leave the assistant living facility against my original wishes. I would soon realize that was a goal cultivated out of fear and safety. But where God was planting me, I would never have to worry about being fearful again Because he would show me what I was truly capable of. That epiphany would be accompanied by a level of overflow I never anticipated or had ever seen before. This my friends were the power of Gods hand and favor. This served as a reminder to me that it did not matter who was against me Because once again God had reminded me that he was always for me! It had been officially three years that I had been a published author, and despite my passion, drive, and work ethic, I had always felt as though I had not received the traction I deserved. Yet now that I was no longer hovering and simply focused on the work itself,

I started to see a change and one I had not anticipated. Suddenly, I was getting offers for speaking engagements, new book reviews from readers, and recognition from people in my community that I wouldn't have expected to be supportive. The irony is that when I hadn't received the support and feedback, I felt a way about it, and now that I was, that also made me feel a way. Although I had received a lot of positive attention and feedback, I couldn't help but notice how uncomfortable that made me feel. Especially when hearing people talk positively about my works and authorship. There I sat doing the work daily, as my passion for writing began to take hold of me more and more, yet there I stood, feeling uncomfortable when my work and talent were acknowledged. I had always felt like people weren't on board in the way I had hoped, yet now that the dynamic was changing, I didn't quite know what to feel, and most times, I felt awkward, in a state of disbelief, or uncomfortable all together as I tried to anticipate what the catch was. This made me realize that all the hate, doubt, and negativity I had experienced over the years regarding my ambitions were much more settled within my psyche than I had hoped. Although I knew I deserved the newfound support and acknowledgment, a part of me couldn't sit amongst it comfortably. Sure, I had done the work to build my business, and I had also been in the home healthcare business since 2009, but it felt unbelievable that the things I had envisioned were coming to be. It also felt good helping people, providing an affordable care option to people in need, and seeing the gratitude and trust people had regarding my business. It always took me very little time to get acclimated on a new case. My new case load had expanded so much there were times I'd be calling clients the wrong names and that was comical to me. People were loving the quality of care my business was offering to their loved ones and I was receiving great feedback from all of my clients. People trusted me so much that my workload started to expand into areas I had never been familiar with. I remember sitting down one day with a client and being trusted with the task of helping him to alter his will. I remember writing out everything he asked me to, emailing it to his lawyer, and family members at his requests and feeling overwhelmed by all of the changes he had me first write and then type in a word document. I noticed as we made more and more progress, he looked overwhelmed. So, I suggested we hold off on pursuing the task, but he declined. He then went on to explain to me why he felt overwhelmed and why completing it that day was of importance to him, and I understood his disposition right away. I offered him some words of solace and he gave me a soft smile and we completed the task. Later that day I reflected on how I was able to help him with a task I initially wasn't comfortable with, but I understood why I had to do it. I also started to understand why God was expanding my work task. Although certain things were not normal for me, I knew my clients needed someone like me because trust is hard to come by and trusting people with your personal life is a huge responsibility. I understood that although I wasn't always comfortable with some of the new requests from my clients it was pertinent that I move forward with the expansion of roles and task Because the industry I was in needed someone like me. This was something the universe kept conveying to me when I would receive feedback and reviews from my new clients. Things had picked up and started moving faster than the speed of lightening but I had been blessed with the ability to keep up with the growth, redevelop myself and my life accordingly, and provide the reality I had envisioned for myself and the people I was serving. I had a few weeks left until my oldest daughter would be eighteen, so I hired her as a companion offering her thirty dollars an hour to sit with a new client, I felt she'd be a great fit for. She started feeling insecure because she had never done anything besides retail but soon enough she realized she had nothing to fear. I had envisioned this for her for so long and I was happy she had started developing an interest on her own. A few weeks prior to me adding her to the team she had sat me down and disclosed to me that she wanted to follow in my footsteps and become a nurse aide, and pursue a PhD in Psychology. That day I felt like I had won the lottery because those were things I felt would be a great fit for her future but I never wanted to be the kind of parent that didn't allow my children to choose for themselves. I was flattered and grateful she was choosing a path I had already envisioned for her. I had set out to offer a customer-centric approach that would allow me to enhance people's lives, and that's what I was doing. I had also set out to write stories where inclusion was the main focal point, people felt inspired, and the black experience swelled within the pages of every novel; that had also been something I had been doing successfully, so it made no sense to feel as though I was an imposter when I was living out my dreams, my visions were flourishing, and I was simply gaining the traction I had earned rightfully. I was finally back to the books and finishing up my last classes to graduate, and my weight loss goals had been met with flying colors. There, I stood a mere 165 pounds after gaining and reaching a weight of 246 pounds. The biggest change that had me feeling the most humbled and overjoyed was the glow-up my seventeen-year-old was experiencing after losing over 90 pounds. Every day, she would work out for an hour to two hours, eat and prep healthy meals, and start presenting herself in a way I loved to see. It made it clear that the fashion girl ascetic I had always known was hereditary. I loved seeing her blossom into the person she always wanted to be physically, and most importantly, I loved the new level of health she had welcomed into her life. We started going on walks together and eventually graduated from walking to jogging. All I could do at times was reminisce on the days we planned to be where we currently were, which felt amazing yet unbelievable. The irony was that when we were both at unhealthy weights, we wore the same size clothes, and after our weight loss goals were met, we were again in the same size clothes. It felt good to set and reach health goals together, but most importantly, it felt good to witness my baby girl feel confident and look how she had always wanted to. Despite the frequent periods of angst we shared, it felt good to be thriving together and seeing our visions manifest into reality, leading me to understand that I was many things, but an imposter was not on that list as I had earned my keep.

CHAPTER 7

Growth Sucks!

My former best friend and I still had not communicated after the project incident, and it had now been a little over a year. Although I had forgiven her and moved on, there were still days when I thought about what she had done, and I found it hard to believe she had handled me the way she had. One day, I logged onto TikTok and decided to play around with the app, hoping to learn how to better maneuver my way around it. I noticed a tiny footprint in the top right corner that I hadn't noticed before. I decided to click on the icon to investigate its function and was floored when I realized it was an icon that allowed me to see who had been viewing my TikTok. At the top of the list sat Raye, who had recently been viewing my TikTok page. The funny thing about people is that no matter what is or isn't, they usually embody the same traits no matter what occurs, and I knew that one view from her would turn into a routine. You see, I knew this because I had watched her fall out with several people, and despite the lack of communication, she made it her duty to keep up with what the people she was exiled from had going on. I found this behavior extremely weird and annoying Because, in my mind, if you don't like a person or have anything good to say about them, what could you gain from tracking their moves? Nonetheless, this was her way, and she knew it was a way that irritated me every time I witnessed her doing it about someone, she claimed to no longer be in communication with. Sure enough, I would check the footsteps icon, and her name would constantly fluctuate, taking her from the middle of my view list to the top daily and weekly, and in my opinion, that shit was pathetic. There she was, my ex-friend of twenty years or more, watching me like a weirdo Because, despite her inability to apologize or simply take accountability for her wrong, she desired to know what I was doing in my life now that she no longer had access to that info and had been blocked on all platforms. Luckily, she came across my TikTok page and quickly reverted to her nosey Nancy Drew ways. It made no sense to me why she couldn't move on from what happened or would be invested in anything that had to do with me, but stupid is as stupid does. I knew she felt bad for what she had done, and I also knew she missed me and wanted to reach out. But I also knew she knew reaching out would be a waste of time because that window had closed. I also knew she was too full of ego and pride to handle things correctly. After all, who waits over a year to right a wrong? In my opinion, a friend who loves and respects you handles you a certain way, and she had made it clear to me that she did not value me, so her stalking my social media was about as close as she was going to get in my space and that was something I was certain she was aware of. After weeks of keeping up with me on TikTok, she started reaching out to my daughter via Snapchat in a way that could seem innocent. Still, I knew Raye and knew she had never taken it upon herself to communicate with my daughter via Snapchat during our relationship; and her attempts felt contrived. But I could also see how that would seem, given how things had gone. My oldest daughter had always had a strong desire to speak her mind and say things that were not always appreciated based on the core component that most of it was filled with truths no one wanted to honor, especially not at the hands of a big mouth teenager who took pleasure in telling it like it was when prompted or triggered. My daughter called me, informing me that Raye had reached out to say happy birthday, and despite it appearing to be an innocent gesture, she didn't feel that way. She then told me how, at the end of her message, she included that my daughter could reach out to her if needed despite the disconnect between her and me. I could've had a field day flooded with commentary about the message, but I knew I didn't need to. My daughter felt a way about the message simply because she, too, felt it was contrived. She highlighted the fact that before that day, Raye had never thought to reach out to her in that way or extend her being there for her Because she felt that she had not been previously in the way she should have as her god mom. I didn't understand why Raye would be stupid enough to reach out to my child, extending her hand knowing that my child was many things, but dumb and gullible was not on the list. What would my child be reaching out to her for? Especially after she had handled her mother in such a foul way. Did she think my daughter would be interested? In my opinion, I don't think she did, but I think she was simply doing what most people in her position do when they have run out of ways to get your attention, and they are not noble enough to say the simple words that need to be said. A simple "I'm sorry for what I did," and she was simply grasping at straws, hoping she could get some form of response from me. Her stating that there was a disconnect was delusional because there was no disconnect. She had shown me with her actions that she had no real care for me, and I honored her behavior by removing myself. This only came as a shock to her because I was the girl who never honored myself over other people. I was also the girl who forgave and forgot at the drop of a dime, so recognizing my worth and not allowing people to play in my face shocked everyone who wanted to get over on me somehow and recognized they couldn't. It had been over a year, and although I felt like she was weird for all of it, I understood the position she was now in. I also understood what led her to do what she did, and despite how hurt I felt, I had silently forgiven her and chosen to move on. The biggest thing was that I had to understand that no one is perfect, not even the people we think the highest of or have the most love for. Because usually, those are the people that let us down. There will always be love in my heart for her because you can't have a long-term relationship as we had and not feel something for the person even after deciding to part ways. I understood that I could not keep holding people to a standard based on what I would and wouldn't do Because that was foolish. I recognized that I wouldn't have handled her that way. Still, I couldn't let that stop me from identifying her behaviors and understanding why I could not continue a relationship with her. I decided to move forward and drop it, which I did. I couldn't let her attempt to cross boundaries. She knew she shouldn't distract me from sticking to what I knew was best for me. It had been extremely hard implementing boundaries with people, even when hurt, and I knew the person I was offering respect to didn't have any for me. It is super easy to lead with hate, anger, hurt, and the list of unfavorable emotions goes on and on. Still, it is hard to lead with love despite not being loved properly, and I was no longer in a space where I was allowing myself to feel like a victim or hold onto things that had already come to pass. This, my friends, is the blessing of real peace and happiness. I was finally sitting in the days of calm that I never knew could truly exist for me, and I was not willing to compromise that space for anyone or anything. So, I did my best and kept focusing on my path, honoring forgiveness and moving forward in the most positive way I could.

Many people were watching me, reaching out to congratulate me on my progress or simply my ability not to give up, and it was appreciated. I remember being in a space where all the views and attention made me feel uncomfortable, and I always had something negative to say about that. Still, I soon realized many people were watching Because I inspired them. Seeing me juggle all these things while being a single mom and a reformed fuck up gave others hope that they, too, could change their lives as I had. I also noticed that once I became truly comfortable with my identity, my thoughts about attention no longer felt uncomfortable or negative. People often reflect on perception as reality but don't speak enough about how it can become skewed based on what is happening inside us. Confidence and self-motivation can be significant blessings when trying to make it through the trenches of life and go after your dreams. I started feeling liberated to love, honor, and believe in myself and my capabilities as a mother, dreamer, creative, and businesswoman. The more I poured into myself, the more the universe filled my cup with unexpected blessings, and that was a wonderful feeling. I had ended many of the relationships in my life, and in the beginning, it felt lonely and confusing for me. Sure, the people I removed had no real respect or care for me, but they were present. Present in a way composed of negative constructs, but sometimes some bad company can feel better than no company at all and that is something many of us latch onto.

Initially, I felt confused and uncertain of my choices because something about making the right choice felt fearful and uncomfortable. Especially when you are first getting started and are unsure if going left is the right option or if you should go right. That's where I was landing mentally on most days. I was out in the wilderness trying to figure out numerous complicated aspects of my life, and all I kept feeling was the constant divide between me and the environment I had known my entire life. I was finally gaining the courage to take a stance and remove what needed to be removed and build what needed to be built, and that, my friends, is a hard journey because you find that the more constructive you become in the realm of polishing up your life to enhance it properly the lonelier you find yourself at times. The gag is that no one tells you that by doing so, you have an amazing opportunity to listen to all the sounds you previously ignored or could never hear. Suddenly, the frequencies started to change, and I became wise to parts of my being that I didn't know existed. God planted me out in the wilderness because he needed me to hear, see, and feel who I was and who I was about to become. With that understanding, I could grow in the areas I needed to and see where I was flawed as a friend, family member, mother, daughter, sister, and so on—that time also allowed me to see all of my beauty and recognize why I was worthy of so many things I had been deprived of. I understood that I sometimes felt the walls caving in on me. My reality was that a group of individuals secretly hated me, despised my ambition, loved seeing me fail, and could not love me properly. That narrative was only true because I had continuously allowed it to be true in my space. I remember growing up hearing older people say that people only do what they know they can do to you, and I was starting to understand why that was true in my case.

So often, I would dissect myself and look at all the components of who I was. I was kind, gentle, helpful, giving, selfless, and catering to a fault. Yet I could also be explosive when pushed to the edge, angry, depressive when prompted by poor treatment, doubtful, insecure, and prone to want to smack the fuck out of someone when triggered in a certain way due to a poor temperament. I could not always control it. Understanding this, I started to sit with myself, dissect, and listen more. I could hear that little girl inside me questioning why love had never been truly given to her, although she knew she deserved it. I could hear that same little girl feeling as if she needed love due to insecurity, rejection, and disappointment. The only love she truly needed was the love she was failing to extend to herself. I could also see that beautiful little girl who was intelligent, driven, and talented feel a lack of worthiness for the things God had already designated as hers because her entire life, people saw her light and made it their business to try and defuse it due to their triggers that stemmed from trauma, and insecurity. I used to wonder what bothered people about me, and in turn, I questioned why so many people could see who I was and feel upset to the point that they wanted to try and invalidate me. The irony is that once I started to understand the power I possessed and allowed God's will more than I tried to understand it, I realized the why was no longer important. Rising above hatred you don't deserve can be extremely hard and mentally taxing. Although I had multiple periods where I felt down and depleted from all the hate energy often propelled in my direction, I knew God was allowing it for a reason beyond my understanding. I also understood how going through those experiences built me to be strong in essential ways, given the path I had chosen to follow. I realized all of my experiences had built me in terms of character. I was developing into the person I needed to be in order to stand firm in the new environments God was planting me in. Environments where I would be responsible for showing up and conducting with the "I think therefore I am" ideology in real time. Environments where my age, race, past history, and single status would not matter as much as my former insecurities would have allowed me to believe. After going through the situations, I had I started becoming smarter, and more determined to become the person God was calling me to be. I understood that all of the uncomfortable experiences I had faced were ingredients designed to redevelop me when sprinkled over my life in the ways God had intended. I could feel myself changing on the inside and it was frightening to say the least. My heart was expanding with intent I had never considered, I was no longer bitter in the ways I thought I should be when analyzing those who had hurt me, and my vision for my life and pursuits were expanding quickly. I could feel that I was on my right path, but I could also feel God merging me into a new person, a person I had formerly been afraid to be out loud. As a psychologist, a mother, a businesswoman, an author, and a motivational speaker, how could I ever reach my goals in these areas and truly help people in the ways I had envisioned if I lacked emotional intelligence? How could I encourage someone as a confidence coach if I were in a space where every time someone said or did something unfavorable to me, I allowed it to shift my confidence? Growth is a troublesome process; the deeper you dive into your growth journey, the more you find infinite challenges. There were many days I wanted to retreat away from the process because it was a significant amount of work, and there were many moments where I felt mentally depleted.

I knew things would not be easy when I decided to make the changes, I knew I needed to, but I didn't anticipate it would be as hard as it had been. Some days, I felt like I would make considerable progress, and something would happen that would pull me back into the space I had graduated from. Finding that growth was often a rollercoaster ride that felt never-ending. Some days, I would meditate and simply ask God, "What in the hell are you doing"? Don't you think I've endured enough? Don't you think I've repeatedly shown my strength to the point that it now feels redundant? Don't you think I deserve a form of resolve not contingent upon this back-and-forth regime? Each time I'd ask these questions, I could only observe his constant response. He'd convey that I needed to be still, have patience, and trust his process despite my discomfort. This constant enlightenment made me realize that no exchange can be offered during a real awakening. God doesn't observe us during our moments of growth and say, hey you, I see you've made some progress, so I'm going to make this journey easier on you! Instead, I believe he says hey, I see you trying; I appreciate your commitment. I will offer you some relief occasionally, but the real deliverance you seek will come at an appointed hour when you no longer watch the clock, feeling entitled due to your commitment. You have come to understand that your process is ultimately in my control, surrender! As a Bonafide control freak, surrendering was the hardest thing for me. What if I surrender and my dreams evaporate, never becoming a reality? What if I surrender and God creates a plan nothing like the visions I hold? I would ponder These types of questions when I thought about letting go and letting God do what he needed for me. Although this response can be a normal human response, when we think about letting go and allowing the universe to do its job, I realize it was a journey I had to honor because no matter how much I wanted to be in control, I knew I was not. I also understood that God had never driven the bus and driven me off into a ditch I couldn't get out of. I recognized that even when I was tossed overboard at times, I always came out better and stronger than before, and that was enough for me to start allowing myself to give in and be still. At times, growth does suck, but I was starting to realize that being a human and an entity who desired control sucked even more! This led me to give up my stronghold on my plans, and I started taking a backseat to life in a way I hadn't before. And once I did this, I found the growth process more interesting than I knew.

CHAPTER 8

Who's That Girl?

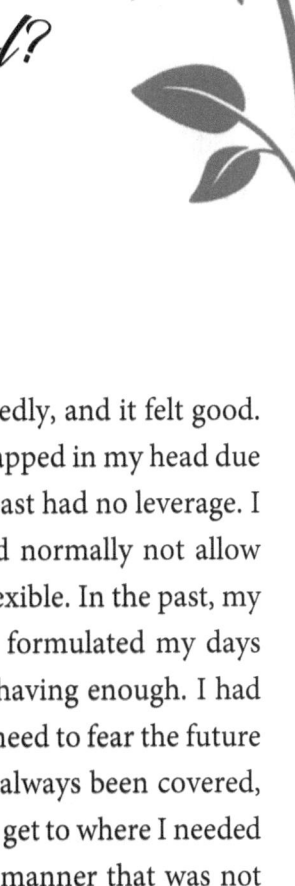

*S*uddenly, life was changing for me unexpectedly, and it felt good. There had been so many days where I felt trapped in my head due to the past, and I was finally in a space where the past had no leverage. I have always been structured, and my OCD would normally not allow much outside the norm, but I was learning to be flexible. In the past, my earning potential usually drove my schedule as I formulated my days around my work because I always worried about having enough. I had now come to the understanding that there was no need to fear the future or worry about not having enough because I had always been covered, and I had always been willing to do the footwork to get to where I needed to be financially when things started to shift in a manner that was not what I desired. I had also realized that less is truly more, and I was starting to feel okay with making financial sacrifices because I knew those sacrifices would pay off eventually.

I left cases that were mentally draining because I was now in a space where my mental health was more valuable than any job or dollar amount. I started taking time off when I felt I could benefit from getting more sleep and putting myself first. This was a huge step in the right direction because, in the past, I had always put my job responsibilities before myself. Ignoring the frequent periods of burnout I would experience, telling myself that there were people relying on me for their well-being and my well-being could wait…which was insane. But you live, and you learn, and I was learning a lot about my behavior patterns and making adjustments that were far beyond my normal scope of improvement.

My body conveyed that it had grown tired and needed more rest. So, as hard as it was for me to slow down, once again, I knew I had no other choice. I dropped the weekend case that required me to work twelve-hour shifts on Saturday and Sunday, reminding myself that sleep was essential. I hated letting my client down because I knew she needed me, and she had not had the best of luck finding caregivers she could connect with, but I also knew my needs were more important at that moment. I knew if I didn't start listening to my body continuously, I would be unable to help anyone, and that was not a path I wanted to take. Suddenly, something clicked on the inside, and I was viewing life with a lighter scope. One that made me feel grateful for the trivial things that were taking place in my life. Some days, I would come home after work, lay in my bed, and look around the room at everything that triggered happy memories. Seeing so many things I had envisioned manifesting in my life felt good, and sometimes it made me tearful. My kids were happy and thriving in ways that required them to stretch themselves and move outside their comfort zones; I was finally at my goal weight, looked as good as I felt, and enhanced my self-care process more than usual. The biggest flex was that I was no longer mentally trapped by old thoughts of poor experiences and past traumas; I had finally come to a place where I felt I had reached a higher level of healing that allowed me to make peace with the past and let it go to strive in the ways I desired. The funny thing is that I remember the days I used to daydream about what life would be like if I had control of my feelings and could push past certain experiences. What amazed me was that I understood that the peace and happiness I desperately needed had been there all along. I had managed to overshadow it by inviting the wrong people into my life, who contributed to having numerous unfavorable experiences that clouded my thoughts and feelings. I was more concerned with the internal components of my being because I finally understood that nothing good happens on the outside until you have created and honored the good on the inside first. Some days, I would come home and become so relaxed and settled that a part of me started to feel as if I was becoming lazy. My naturally busy body behavior could not calmly accept my body's newly formed foundation that was co-dependent on frequent rest periods and the desire to be still and only move when it was vital. I was getting better at being less hard-headed and retracting from my keen ability to learn the hard way. I told myself that if I paid attention to my body before I felt drained, I would make more progress in all areas of my life. This was when I started asking myself questions and analyzing aspects of my personality that still needed adjusting. As a go-getter and a single mother, it is often common for a woman to feel that slowing down would be a disservice. Several times in my life, I felt this was true until I started viewing things through a new lens. I wondered about taking a day off. That seemed so wrong. Why did it often feel like self-care days took away time that I felt could be used more constructively? Was sleep also an important construct for one to thrive physically and mentally? I realized that my inability to rest stemmed from a place of fear and self-doubt because my biggest fear was always not making it to the finish line. This never made sense to me because I was a serial goal-Reacher, an organized routine freak, and highly consistent. I noticed that the more I meditated, operated outside of a space of hyperarousal behaviors, and got the proper rest, the clearer my thoughts, intent, and outcomes were. I also loved the time I had with my kids because I did not have much free time while working the insurance job, and my leaving that career opened my vortex to many opportunities with my children. Some days, I would look at my children and Basque in gratitude for seeing how far God had brought us all in such an abbreviated time. I had been the girl to accept maltreatment from romantic partners, family, and friends. I had been the girl to give more than I received. I had also been the girl who, due to a lack of awareness, self-love, and past trauma, allowed my trauma to create trauma for my children due to them witnessing the poor experiences I had previously allowed. Although it pained me deeply to own the flawed nature of the past, it brought me immense joy to assess the strength, growth, and joy we were walking into gracefully. I had been the girl to accept so many poor behaviors from others and myself. Despite that truth, I was now the woman who knew her worth, didn't waste her time, and released the past, and I was also the woman who was contributing to the healing and betterment of three children. Children who, despite me letting them down previously, had forgiven my flaws, loved me unconditionally, and viewed me as a hero even when I felt the sting of failure knocking at my backdoor. Previously, if the question had arisen and someone wanted to inquire who's that girl? My response would have been one I was embarrassed by. Now, I could respond to the inquiry with diligence and strength after having prevailed despite my former belief that I could not.

CHAPTER 9

Sowing Seeds

*I*t had been a year since I had released my last two publications, and due to time constraints, grief, and fear, I hadn't done much since releasing the books. It had been a long time since I had done any type of interview or speaking engagement, and although I had a silent desire to get back up on the horse and put myself back out there, I had so many things on my plate that I felt exposure could wait. It had been almost three years since I became a published author, and my creativity portal had recently expanded. I was now on my way to enhancing the expectation of two books per year to four, and that was a goal I was excited about and afraid of fulfilling simultaneously. Although I knew it would be important for me to start doing engagements again to bring awareness to my projects, it was not something I was in a rush to do for obvious reasons. I learned that when God is ready for you to move, he will move you despite your reservations. A representative from one of the local libraries contacted me inquiring if I would like to be a part of a speaker panel of authors for the local writers group. I hadn't done anything in a while and told myself the event would be the perfect opportunity to return to the horse. On the day of the event, I arrived at the library and met two great authors who were also there to speak about their experiences as writers. I sat at the table, preparing for my old nemesis' anxiety to show up. To my surprise, anxiety was nowhere to be found. The authors all started giving their spill of expertise, and I sat listening feeling empowered by hearing them share new knowledge, what had and had not worked for them, as well as empowering dialect to help inspire the aspiring authors who all sat wide-eyed and focused on the table across from us. To my surprise, there were many questions about fiction writing and self-publishing, and I spoke more than I had anticipated. Yet when I opened my mouth to respond, no nervous energy was present. Where had my anxiety gone? Why was my larynx no longer shaking like a broke stripper? Where was all of the passion in my response coming from? There I sat, allowing myself to be vulnerable as I shared with the group the many disheartening experiences I had faced as a new author, what I had learned, and why creating the visions you see in your mind was important. Suddenly, the fear of rejection and criticism had left me, and I was allowing myself to be what I already was without being sidetracked by doubt. I went home that day observing that the more I wrote, the more my love of writing was inflated. I remember being in a space where I wanted to start writing, but I didn't know how or if I should. The irony is that I was now in a space where I couldn't imagine a world where I did not write because it was now a huge part of my existence. It also gave me a liberating feeling, allowing me to occasionally escape my busy, loaded reality. On my iPhone, I had compiled a list of over 70 book titles and concepts of books I planned to write and publish. Week after week, I found myself thinking of new creative projects and adding them to the list. I promised myself that I would write and publish every idea that came to mind and write and write and write until I had disposed of every literary vision on my long list. I thought about my heightened creativity over the past three years. The process that started with the compilation of one creative vision was now a vision that consisted of almost one hundred book ideas, all that stemmed from my imagination, and that was a beautiful epiphany. Day after day, I observed myself morphing into the creator I always dreamed of being, and it was a blessing to acknowledge that in a space where outside validation or gratification was not present. It's amazing how powerful the mind can be when we allow ourselves to shut out the noise and dive into our process. I remember the days when I used to observe other creators and wonder how it was; they had so many ideas come to them. I never anticipated the day my idea vortex would open up, and multiple literary visions would flow to me effortlessly, waiting to be brought into my reality. I started to value my imagination more and more because I understood it was the portal to a beautiful existence of purpose and passion. I initially started my journey as a writer wanting to create fictional, magical novels where inclusion was present. Novels that walk the reader through a supernatural journey filled with realism, culture, comedy, and relatable experiences. Although that goal had not changed, I started observing how my vision for my work expanded every time I wrote. Every time I sat down to create a new manuscript, there was a feeling present that I noticed every time but couldn't put into words. There was also a new feeling of surprise that struck me each time I read over my work, instantly observing the growth in my writing. I felt surprised by the development in my work, but I felt even more surprised at my ability to pull from my imagination and take an idea that was once just a thought and then a title and create a three-hundred-page manuscript. Filled with life, created with love, and fueled by my heightened imagination. I thought about all the times in the past when I doubted myself and my capabilities. Have you ever looked back over your life and thought if only I knew back then what I know now? There were several times I wanted to kick myself for not getting an earlier start on certain things. Still, I also understood that if I had gotten an earlier start, there was a possibility I would have ruined my journey due to where I was mentally during the earlier days of my life. One night, I arrived at work ready to work the night shift. I got everything I would need to have a successful sixteen-hour shift. I made my first round on the floor, ensuring all the residents were in their beds safely. I plugged up my phone and laptop and prepared to make my rounds developing the five manuscripts I was working on. I sat at my desk typing away, weaving in and out of one magical text to the next, pushing myself to get the things onto paper that was brewing in my head impatiently. The call bell rang, alerting me that it was time to retreat from my manuscript and attend to work. I looked at the screen and noticed it was Jack Maroon. Jack was one of my favorite residents at the facility, and he was also an intelligent man who held a PhD and was a former computer science professor who had pushed to enhance the number of women and minorities who enrolled in the computer science program. I entered the room, greeting Jack, trying to assess what he needed. He told me his granddaughter had read The Diary of Janay Wilkerson twice and loved the book. He began inquiring when book two would be available, insisting I keep him updated so he could purchase book two for her. This warmed my heart and made me happy that a young reader enjoyed the book. As a writer, you never know how your work will be perceived, and the Diary of Janay Wilkerson had several flaws within the text, so it made me feel overwhelmed with happiness anytime I learned of a reader who had an appreciation for the text. There I stood again, humbled and happy to be sowing seeds of creativity I could share with the world while on a lifelong journey to build, inspire, and create change through my creations.

CHAPTER 10

Elevation with a Side of Misinterpretation

*I*t had been almost two years since I decided to part ways with Raye after being best friends for over twenty years. After coping with the experience and demise of our long-term relationship, I had decided, like usual, that it was only right to go back into hermit crab mode. After all, how could I trust anyone enough to start forging new relationships when things had gone the way they had with me and Raye? Hadn't I endured enough at this point? Was it worth it? It was no secret that I had allowed the negative experiences I had encountered to keep me from creating new positive experiences simply because I had told myself there was no real resolve for me. Of course, I wanted to create new relationships that did not require me to water myself down, but a huge part of my existence felt like that was not possible. I was tired of trying to make light of uncomfortable situations and walking into situations where I unconsciously triggered other people's insecurities by simply being myself. It frustrated me when I observed the many people who knew what I had been through and saw my struggles firsthand. Yet, they had somehow managed to hate me for my progress and strong will that always allowed me to overcome every battle, no matter how complex. People often try and glorify empowered women, but they never offer you the truth in terms of how uncomfortable things can be for the empowered woman who has decided to overcome her environment. The irony was I had started to see that some form of adversity would always be brewing in the midst, whether I welcomed it or not. Growth was just as problematic as stagnancy, and this was a dynamic I hated experiencing simply because it left me feeling like people wanted to punish me for growing past their expectations. I was once again allowing my fear to get the best of me, but I would soon meet new people who would remind me that there were still good people left in the world despite the negative thought process I had been clinging to that informed me otherwise. My business had started growing, but I was still working full-time at an assisted living facility, constantly meeting new people. Working at the facility helped me to grow in terms of my communication skills. I started finding it easy to talk and interact with people, and suddenly, I was back to my old self again. I didn't realize it until one day; I was instantly thrown off when I overheard a coworker describe me as a people person. There had to have been a disconnect. How was I being described in such a way after having been in hermit crab mode since my trauma? Once again, God stepped in and decided to send me yet another resource he knew I needed at the current moment that I was unaware of. It was no secret that I had always been comfortable standing alone, never feeling like I needed others in my space to feel content. But I wasn't ready to own that we all need people in our space to thrive in a healthy way conducive to a healthier mental stance, which I had been lacking due to the sting of old experiences. I had met many people while working at the facility, but only two of them stood out to me as contacts I would feel comfortable utilizing outside of work. Kiana and Alexis were two co-workers I was starting to get more and more comfortable communicating with despite my anxiety. Alexis was about eight years older than me and a Leo like my mother. From day one, when she started on the night shift, she and I connected immediately; it was like we had known one another for years. Kiana was a few years younger than me, and she and I also clicked right away. The irony is that so much about Kiana reminded me of Raye. It made it clear that I preferred certain energy within my social networks. Kiana invited me to a concert and agreed that Alexis could accompany the group. This got things rolling in a different direction because I had not been in the spirit of trying to make friends since the event with Raye had occurred. But it was easier forging bonds with these two ladies simply because it felt natural like I had known them forever. After agreeing to go to the concert with the girls, I went online to order my outfit and shoes and was getting prepared to go have some much-needed fun with a new group of women. Suddenly, my old nemesis anxiety crept in, and I started having opposing thoughts about my new friends. What if I went and they turned out to be just as phony and envious as the women I had previously befriended in my past? Suddenly, my thoughts started to fail me, and I started feeling plagued by one intrusive thought after another. All of which were of a negative origin concerning this new girl group I was infiltrating my way into naturally. I decided the best way to help myself overcome my negative thought process so I could continue making progress with my new friends was to be open and honest about where I was internally and why. I informed Kiana that the real reason I had flaked on going to the concert with her was my anxiety, and I told her that I had been to myself for a long time after being betrayed by numerous people. It felt impossible to abandon my negative thought processes concerning building new bonds. After coming clean with Kiana about my experiences in friendship and how it had cultivated a culture of fear and anxiety for me, she expressed that she, too, had been through some issues with a friend and was no longer communicating with her. Hearing her disclose her experiences where her friend exhibited jealousy and hatred led me to understand that we had much more in common than I had originally understood. It made me realize how common my relationship experiences were within my community. She was extremely comical, stylish, hardworking, and outspoken, which I greatly appreciated. It felt good to reach a place in my life that I previously thought would not come. Just a year ago, I had told myself I wouldn't ever find new friends simply due to my habits of staying in the house and my dire ability to allow my anxiety to lead the way. Just like that, I had gained traction with new people, being my former outgoing self, planning friend dates and girls' trips, and allowing the new bonds I created to grow despite my fear of the future. For the longest time, I had been a prisoner of my own mind due to the constant hateful energy I would receive from the people within my environment. This caused me to take on avoidance behaviorism due to my constant doubt. I would often try to dissect what it was about me that made others so bothered, angry, bitter, jealous, and petty, and the list would go on and on. There I stood daily, trying to focus on my own plate. I tried to cultivate a life that would allow me to be the best mother, daughter, sister, and achiever I could be because, in reality, those were the only things that were important to me. I didn't understand how my aspirations, progress, or behavior could upset someone, especially when striving to be the person I felt God was calling me to be. Nothing about who I was had changed internally. Sure, my outward aesthetic had evolved regarding the physicality of the culture of living I had cultivated, but I was still the same Nina. I was still the Nina who loved to make people laugh, spoke her mind whenever prompted, cared about everyone more than she cared about herself, was ambitious, shy, hardworking, opinionated, loyal to a fault, and understanding. I was also still the Nina afraid of her own potential, insecure about the light that made others feel uncomfortable, too forgiving, with a poor temperament that often skewed my ability to uphold emotional intelligence when triggered. I was starting to understand that I could truly be myself and not worry about the pushback I received from people who didn't know me, had never had a conversation with me, and were interpreting me based on the opinions of others or the valor they extracted from my social media platforms. One of the main commonalities I had started to notice was all of the awkward components that were starting to show up in my life anytime I tried to make an additional improvement and stand on my capabilities. I started to understand the disservice I was offering to my reality every time I critiqued myself in an overbearing way, doubted the capabilities I knew existed within me, and fed into the outside world that constantly wanted to place me in a box. I started wondering what makes the world want to confine the black woman to so many statistical spaces despite her ability to show the world that she is thriving and does not belong in a defined space. Why is it that we are not allowed to be smart, funny, outgoing, ambitious, independent, creative, agile, submissive, stern, catering, caring, and powerful without others making us feel as though we have to pay a toll to a world that wants to make us feel that if we encompass too many things at once we should therefore be considered "too much." Society teaches us that the black woman can not be filled internally with multiple traits of excellence without her having to subject herself to a world that will teach her that because she has overcome misplaced stigmas and crossed the threshold that was never supposed to be compromised, she must now be spoon fed crumbs within her existence. Crumbs that allow her to believe she cannot have a certain type of circle because the world says all black women are competitive and jealous hearted regarding one another. The crumbs that allow her to believe she must settle for the lackluster relationship that comes with a black man who is making less money, less educated, and less interested in upholding her to a space of prominence where she can be made to feel safe, respected, and nurtured in the way she deserves and desires. Then there are the crumbs that convey to the black woman that she must be a "ride or die" candidate in terms of the way she faces life. Teaching her that she has to endure struggle because there is no happy peaceful existence for her unless there are struggle components within her relationships, finances, or overall capability to create a life indulged with purpose. To make it plain and simple, I was tired of entering spaces where it was clear to me that people felt as though my only right to be in the space, I was currently inhabiting could be based on my aptitude to lessen the blow of my existence by muting myself in spaces where people did not understand or interpret me correctly. This always allowed me to revert back to a mental space of exploration that would lead me down a path where I consistently probed my way through the past, comparing in contrast how it was always easier for me when I wanted nothing, achieved less, and was failing more based on poor decision-making skills. This skewed expectation allowed me to understand the importance of living my truth no matter who that truth disrupted. I told myself I would never again allow the world to place me in a box because I knew God had not blessed me with the ability to discover and interpret myself in depth for me to turn around and compact and confine my true nature. This realization helped me start to own who I was and who I was becoming. I started relying on my emotional intelligence to help me consider that the overall truth in terms of my being misinterpreted was not something I needed to care about. Based on the understanding that I had cultivated a new life allowing me to see that most of the inappropriate behaviors distributed in my direction based on my stance had nothing to do with me. And that discovery alone was freeing because it allowed me to take up space and be unapologetic. It frustrated me that people's perceptions were never fueled with accuracy. I wondered what it was about the black woman and her unanticipated growth that led her constituents to feel plagued and disrespected by her glow-up. What about her made others want to brand her as a pretentious snob with the nerve to evolve in the open amongst observers who did not want, respect, or value her transition? While viewing her with an envious scope as they probe their way through the Million Dollar question that was often asked secretly. Who does she think she is? If I ever had the opportunity to answer, I would say she thinks she is the answer to the generational curses that have been unconsciously handed down generously within her lineage since the beginning of time. She thinks she is the woman who has been through trauma, did the shadow work to heal, and has cultivated an understanding that life does not have to be filled with the struggles of her previous environment. I think the irony that has always been the most disturbing to me is the ideology that there is no real win when you are in certain types of environments. People will attack, taunt, and talk about you for being anxious, unaware of your Presence, and speak against you for owning the insecurities they have placed upon your being. Yet if you have the favor and ability to rise above those kinds of mental and environmental subjections and decide to be stern in who you are by loving yourself to the fullest capacity, embracing your intellect, and understanding your environment to the point you can interpret the outcome long before you hear, see, or experience anything leading to a mental disruption you are deemed a problem. Leading me to deduce that no matter which road you decide to travel, there will always be misinterpretations along the way, so you might as well travel the road of empowerment and enlightenment. The road that leads you to a prominent space where you can fully understand yourself enough to own your talents and capabilities, give back to the world by pouring into others through the goodness that God has diligently poured into you free of charge, and live out loud. So, when you are faced with this million-dollar question again in real-time, and someone inquires, "Who does she think she is?" you can answer, "I am the woman God has created me to be!"

CHAPTER 11

Betrayal is the Blessing!

T hings were finally falling into place for me and all the people around me at once. My brother Melvin Jr. Had stepped into his new career position and was now thriving at the speed of lightning and it made me proud. He had stepped headfirst into his role, learned faster than the average human would thanks to his abnormal IQ and ability to process complex information. His roles were expanding fast, and he was now stepping into mentoring roles right after coming out of mentorship, being prepped for leadership, and earning well beyond six figures while saving and planning to purchase his first home. Gavin was doing well in the position he had been in for years and was now working towards career advancement, moving into a bigger home, and traveling around the world experiencing new countries frequently. This was a beautiful sight to witness for me as the oldest sibling simply because I knew the things we had all gone through in our lives that had stripped us of our essence at times, hardened our scope, and made us feel as though we could not be better than the environments we had come to know within our childhood. But babyyyyyy let me be the first to say that God had been doing his big one regarding my loved ones and once he put his foot to the petal he never let up. It feels good to win but it is an even better feeling to win in unison and that's where he had decided to plant us. We had gone through so much together and so much apart from one another and our new lives reflected so much strength, agility, and favor. My mother had been a single mother all those years doing it by herself and at times she made it look so damn easy that one could deduce due to common ignorance that it had been, but that had never been the case. It wasn't until I became a single mother that I was able to truly reflect on my mother's hardships, and triumphs and get a feel for what it was she had truly endured and overcame successfully. My brother Melvin had been traveling a lot for work and had recently been deployed in Hawaii for an extended work stay. One day he sent me photos that caused me to break into a deep reflective moment as I thought about all that God was doing in his life and Gavins's life and it brought me to tears. Some would argue that the tears were simply because I have always been a crybaby by nature while some would agree that the reflective moment allowed me to view Gods hand and promise in our lives. It was no secret we didn't come from much and our mother was the truest definition of "getting it out the mud" that we had ever witnessed. I thought about how a few years ago me and Gavin would travel a lot together, but we would go to places that were sensible for us at that time like Vegas or Miami never really thinking beyond those types of locations. Yet a few years later we were now planning trips out of the country frequently , and expanding our culture vortex by joining each other in environments we would have never thought we would have the ability to experience. So many things were coming together for me and my family all at once that helped me to understand the importance of preparation. Sure, when things hit you can get ready but isn't the goal always to do less work? Why should there be a preparation period incorporated into your now when you can prepare for the now so that when it shows up there is no extra work or logistics that need to be focused on. I had started to feel my intuition tugging at me telling me to "get ready". What I was getting ready for I did not quite know, but nonetheless I knew I was hearing this message. Although I had still been struggling with anxiety and the negative drawbacks from my anxious feelings, I knew it was pertinent that I continue trying to push past it and force myself to show up in the ways I knew I needed to but previously could not. I started reaching out to people within the community to inform them of my business, my vision for community service components I could offer, as well as inquire about opportunities to make connections with others who were in my field or in fields where they offered some form of care or assistance to others. Each time I reached out to someone new I felt as if I was holding my breath underwater and needed to come up for air. I soon started to realize that despite my anxious feelings I was a better communicator than what I understood myself to be. I was pitching my business, goals, and hopes to complete strangers and watching as they all responded back to me in a positive way shifting my outer reality. Allowing me to stray away from the previous notion of thinking everyone would be as negative or passive aggressive as others had been in my past. I had experienced some unfavorable events; the past still held no place in my present or my future. I was starting to understand the power of letting things go and letting God drive the bus. Whatever had happened to me had already occurred, and those events may have prompted me to shed some tears, feel bitter, feel belittled, and often feel out of place within my day-to-day world. But those same events had led me to understand my strengths, weaknesses, and essentially my ability to thrive and overcome despite the many storms that were brewing in my direction. It's hard to let go when you feel you've been wronged but sometimes the process can become easier when you view betrayal and heartbreak from a different angle. I had watched a video where someone spoke about the things that build us to be our best selves. During the video the speaker highlighted how although it can be deemed cliché at times "the betrayal was the blessing". Naturally upon hearing this I initially felt like the statement itself was bogus. How could someone stabbing me in the back be a positive notion when it had caused me so much negativity within my life. I started to dissect the ideology of that statement, comparing certain events against one another. Silently deducing quickly how the statement was absolute in most scenarios. My ex-husband treating me the way he did permitted me to step into my true essence as a woman allowing me to recognize the quality of woman I am and what it is I deserve. It also helped me to recognize how much I tried muting myself within that relationship only to try and fit in with a class of individuals who were on a lower level of life than me in terms of the way they thought, acted, and treated others. My friend betraying me after all those years allowed me to understand how I put people upon pedestals who didn't deserve it, how I overlooked people doing corrupt acts to others telling myself "Yeah that's pretty fucked up, but my friend won't ever do something like that to me". Only to turn around and be shocked when that same level of grim was propelled in my direction. I realized I had watched certain friends get things by illegitimate means, steal, lie, scheme, and hate on people who were doing it the honest way. These same friends would act and speak a certain way and I would disregard it based on my people pleasing tendencies that I was not fully aware of at the time. You see I was the queen of speaking my mind but when it came to my loved ones, I was gentler with the truth especially when I knew the truth was a hard pill for them to accept. The irony is most times these same people who I constantly tried to shield and protect from harsh truths had no problem dishing it out in my direction. My innate nature had always been that of a caregiver and a provider and although I was a girly girl the caregiver/ provider role I had been forced to take on during my early years had morphed me into an alpha female with big D energy! My masculine behavior was often unmatched and made me a hard act to follow for most men. Because I often found myself running into the man with low key feminine energy like my ex-husband. Men who couldn't provide shit but community penis, lies, and a keen ability to want a woman to protect, and provide based on their mother's inability to do so for them as children. Or I would have the privilege of running into a full-grown man who found my outer aesthetic pleasing but was turned off by my inner aesthetic that consisted of a woman with a strong mind, a big ass mouth, stubbornness that had been unmatched by most, and an independent way that was not attractive to the man who wanted a soft, gentle woman he could take care of. I realized my poor relationships had all taught me so much, and I had learned who it is I am by learning from being who it was I did not want to be. I started rethinking how I felt about what Raye had done and I realized why God had allowed it. That situation helped me to learn how to be a better friend to myself, during my period of alone time. It also helped me learn how to own red flags when I recognized them within my loved ones and within myself. I also realized that I had been a people pleaser trying to shield the people I cared about from truths they needed to be aware of. I had never known a middle ground within most things but lately I was becoming flexible in ways I had not anticipated. I realized I could still be my normal big mouth self and speak my truth to people without hurting their feelings deliberately. The moral of every story within my life that I had explored relayed to me how the deceit was a necessary part of my journey, and it taught me how to not only be better to myself, build better relationships, but also take account of the roles I played in all of it by allowing things I didn't deserve. I had watched how so many people had thrived off of celebrating my discomfort and hurt but those same people were now being made to sit in on a chapter of my life they were all to ignorant to anticipate. A chapter filled with knowledge, clarity, ownership, building, thriving, and succeeding in ways they hated to bear-witness to. All the people who had let me down were now viewing me turn my life into everything they hoped I would not. Although I had been working towards certain things with some of these people present in my life at times, I realized why it had never fully manifested when they were present. They were not my people, and I was not ready for the things I was currently manifesting back then. I had built traction in the past and then I would turn around and self-sabotage my experience based on my keen ability to do so during those days. I would then turn around and blame the people I was around for my mishaps for the roles they played in it when in reality they were not at fault. I was! I saw all of these people for who they truly were, what they were capable of, and most importantly the low-key hate they had for me that was not as low key as they thought. But I kept these people close allowing them to do the things they did because I was afraid of myself. Afraid of what it would look like if I grabbed the level of success I saw in my dreams. I was fearful of bringing my many visions to life because what if I was meant to have, be, and do all these things? How would I respond to that kind of increase? Who would I have around? I had witnessed how most people will hate you, wish bad for you, and leave you for having and being a lot less. The truth was I had become comfortable with shady low-key hatred because it was all I had known my entire life. How could I be around people who actually liked me? How could I enjoy it without constantly seeing negative components of their being because my past had taught me that most people would view me as too much! And most people would find me pretentious, overdressed, and overly ambitious. But I was now owning a new reality that conveyed to me that even if someone was thrown off when meeting me, they would find me intriguing in a positive way, hardworking, diligent, funny, and fashionable. I started spinning my former ways of thinking and just like that my reality started to reflect those positive thoughts I was having to reshape daily. People had been horrible to me but not all people are horrible. I had been horribly afraid of myself but there was no reason for me to fear the portions of who I was that could be deemed misunderstood. I was a talker and I spoke with an elevated since of knowledge, vulnerability, and truth most would be too afraid to, but that was a gift from God. I was always overdressed but I was and had always been a fashion girl who viewed clothes as a form of art! I was also creative, passionate, and I visualized dreams that made sense for who I was on a normal basis and that was also of God. I was learning to be unapologetically me in every room I entered. I was also learning to ditch my worries about how I would be received because the people who were meant to see me were and those who misinterpreted me didn't matter. The funny thing about assignments is that they link us to others who also have assignments to carry out and often we don't realize how many links God has put in place for us to see to it that we carry out the assignments he has obligated to us! Those people who laughed at me, talked about me, doubted me, or simply just didn't understand me were not supposed to. They were chains linked to my process that were put in place to help me learn to see myself, move forward without any push or support, and help me to cultivate my visions by helping me to place my complete trust in God and myself! With such a daunting assignment I was finally understanding why things were what they were and why. Clarity is a beautiful yet painful blessing that opens your eyes to the areas you may have been blind to before. My many mental explorations to the past helped me to own the understanding that the betrayal is always the blessing!

CHAPTER 12

Abundance is Here!

The more I kept my thoughts aligned with positivity the more I was starting to witness my reality transition in a positive way. I encountered a lot of new people and built connections which was something new for me. Although I had always been introverted in my way, I was starting to see how letting people in was not always a negative experience. I had gotten a new full-time case at a facility and had been working on the case for a little over three months. Every day I would enter the building and watch as everyone looked at me trying to make sense of my overdressed aesthetic. Soon-after they'd smile, and compliment something I was wearing, and I was not used to that. This was the daily exchange for me every day I came to work, and it was something that made me feel good. Not because of the compliment, because I liked clothes and they made me look and feel-good daily, but it felt good to finally walk into an environment and not feel I was being judged in a negative way because of my fashion sense. People in the past used to try and make me feel bad for wanting to look my best. But once again God was teaching me to keep showing up as myself because somewhere there were environments where who I am was permissible! I walked in meetings dressed to impress, booked contracts, and built business connections without having to dull down my choice in clothing, hair, or nail art. Every time I allowed someone the opportunity to get to know Nina, they learned fast that Nina was more than what met the eye. Leading others to respond to my essence outwardly showing appreciation for the parts of my being I used to think I needed to mute to see results or avoid negative behaviors from others. God was saying to me that it was okay for me to live out loud because there were plenty of people who could benefit from me and my offerings. It was clear to me there were certain people who waited for me to walk through the door just to see what look I'd be giving that day and it had now become a thing. I wasn't used to so many women showing me love, smiling when they viewed my look, or just simply allowing me to be me and it felt good. Especially when I could respond and share what cheap website, I purchased the item from and have them reply sharing a cheap fashion tip in exchange. These conversations started to lead to more in depth conversations with women who like usual would pour out there deepest, realest experiences to me. Allowing me to listen as they shared their accounts of poor marriages, abuse, and insecurities. Allowing me to take it in, offer them verbal solace, and share how I understood based on my own experiences with situations like those they were encountering. I remember one woman approaching me with her truth after learning about Baltimore Imprint and sharing her account of marital abuse with me and sharing how after overcoming twenty years of abuse she was now in a new happy healthy marriage. She then inquired about my life asking me if I was dating anyone. I shared with her that I had been single and celibate since the end of my marriage and had no desire to date due to anxiety that I was still trying to overcome. I expressed to her that building trust in a relationship would not be ideal for me at that moment. Well, how long has it been? she asked, still looking at me confused. Over two years I replied watching as her face balled up with disagreement. "Hunny don't let that man ruin it for the next man, you are too young for all that" she continued as she viewed me in disbelief. It didn't make sense to her that I was walking around looking like a snack, yet no one had taken a bite for so long! The exchange was extremely comical to me because I knew it didn't make much sense to me either. But what can you do when your body has the appeal, but your brain is uninterested in exploring intimacy? I hadn't been able to get passed the mental components that needed to be altered for me to even consider dating but I knew when the time was right God would help me overcome my fears that surrounded love and intimacy. My days were still the same, revolving around motherhood, growth, and my goals. I was still working a lot more than the average human and I had started falling more and more in love with my job at the assisted living community where I worked. I had requested to be transferred to the memory care unit and after falling in love with the people and the way things went, I knew I had found a permanent place for myself. I was consistently picking up overtime and the feeling I got when coming to work was one that was familiar to me. It was the same feeling I had when showing up to Dr Braxtons each day. The feeling the came along with knowing my work was making a difference for someone. I had stopped taking the steps that were necessary to build up my clientele for my business and I had gone back to working for other agencies. After taking a break to get acclimated to my new job, things kept occurring that highlighted that I was not on the right path. So, I took heed and started back making marketing material, putting up yard signs in different areas, and reaching out to facilities in the area to inform them about my agency. I have always been a firm believer in the phrase "where focus goes, energy flows" and just like that energy was back flowing in the direction of my business. After gaining a new case the facility where I had been working on the case for a few months recommended my agency to someone and a few days later I had another new case. My plan was to Stay at the assistant living facility I was at until I acquired my PhD. Although I was happy for the increase of abundance for my business I was afraid how the roles, hours, and responsibilities would affect my job at the facility. Shortly after both cases increased the hours and I was no longer available in the ways I usually was on the weekend leaving me unable to do my normal fifteen-hour shifts at the facility on the weekend. For a second, I started spiraling in thought before cutting my negative thoughts short and reminding myself that anything taken from me was no longer meant to be a part of my life. Then I started following what God was telling me to do and I quit the agency I had been working for that had been my safety net/ backup plan just in case things didn't work out. I informed my job of the changes in my life and to my surprise they removed me from the schedule for the hours I could not work, and they allowed me to stay on full time and pick up when and as much as I wanted. There was a huge part of me that feared it would go a different way because I had been so used to people trying to take from me once my increases started to arrive. God was showing me that I was allowed to grow in all the ways I desired without people holding it against me. I was starting to encounter people who were smitten by my way and didn't want to punish me for it. People who didn't know my story but respected my hustle and intellect in a way I was not familiar with. And it felt good because it was helping me to try and dispose of my fears when I could. I didn't become fear/ anxiety free, but I started making small strides consistently that were helpful to me in many areas of my life. After seeing my business rise again I started putting in the work to be consistent in areas like marketing and building my buissness contacts because those were the areas, I hated but I knew building those components could be very beneficial for me as a buissness woman. I started meeting other woman who did the kind of work I was doing who could benefit from coming to work for me and I started taking contact info anytime my Spidey senses went off and I found myself in the midst of a good caregiver who encompassed the right qualities. I remember meeting two women and seeing them in leadership roles on cases instantly and offering them pitches abruptly to see if coming to work for me would be of interest to them. I told myself I would stay ready at all times because things were picking up and I was no longer going to slow down out of fear when things picked up in my life because increase was something I deserved, and I had been putting in the work to obtain abundance, so I needed to stop trying to flee away from the experience out of fear of the unknown. Life had never been predictable for me and it probably never would be but I was tired of being afraid of my cup when it overflowed because that was always the goal! That overflow was the very thing that had allowed me to be a blessing to so many people in my life . Only difference is this time I would be blessing a different genre of people and building change in a way that was not connected to my friends or family but to a large pool of strangers who needed my offerings to get through the day. My kids were all experiencing different changes as always I felt like motherhood always tugged me in a million emotional directions at once. Whether it was my youngest going through an anxious episode and crying because she would have much rather been home with me every day to stay free of anxiety, my son clinging to his video game and feeling ok with only engaging with the people in his household, or my oldest going through mental tangents due to her own uncomfortable feelings about her glow up and how her peers were responding to her because of it, I had a full load. I kept informing Kylie that negative and positive responses were all a part of the glow-up experience. I encouraged her not to take in much about either response in order to keep a level head. She had decided she wanted to try and branch out a little more and disclosed to me how she had been invited to a school cookout by one of her male peers. I did a deep dive and learned he was the leader of the black student union and had many other positive qualities, so I felt it was safe to let her go. I dropped her off at the cookout and came back to pick her up. I felt frustrated as she left me sitting in the car for an elongated period like I had become her willful uber driver. Which couldn't have been possible simply because I had cursed and complained about taking her and coming to get her. I viewed her through my rear-view mirror walking toward me slowly as if She thought I was on her time and had nowhere to be. I prepared my voice box for the yelling session I was going to give her as soon as she sat in the seat of my car. I watched as she paused and a young man walked up to her talking to her unaware that if he held her up a minute longer, he was going to become her taxi home. I watched as she gave him her number and instantly my anger became lessoned by me witnessing the event. She hopped in the front seat apologetic about how long she had taken before diving right into all of the details about the cookout and the young man I had watched through the mirror. After listening to her I had forgotten how mad I was and it sent me somewhere else entirely. My Babygirl was growing up and it was heartwarming watching her grow into herself and face her fears. A few weeks later she went on her first date with the young man. He accompanied her on a picnic at the lake down the street from our house and although I was at work, I rushed home on my break to meet him. He was polite, respectful, and handsome and he didn't mind me snapping pictures of them together while Kylie complained about me hovering and embarrassing her. "Oh my god mom, do you have to?" she asked as I snapped pictures taking notice of how they looked related due to their complexions and curly hair texture. "It's okay my mom would probably have done the same thing," Cameron said as he assured me my parachute ways were okay with him. A few weeks later she was in her first relationship, and it was such a moment for me and her. She was stepping into so much happiness within her life and building new healthy connections and it made me so overwhelmed with joy and frequent tears. It was so unbelievable to me how fast time had passed. We were now walking in the days we had dreamed about for her and it felt good seeing her glow and growth.

CHAPTER 13

Hicks Casserole with a Side of Goddard Pie

Throughout my thirty-five years on this planet, I have come to learn so many things that have heightened my human experience. I've also had the privilege of consistently stumbling upon information that has been helpful to me during many trying periods in my life. Positive affirmations, meditation, and speaking seminars, where some of my favorite inspirational muses advised about manifesting, were a weekly regimen that kept me going. On an extremely hard day, I would gravitate to YouTube and listen to Steve Harvey, Les Brown, Oprah, and Louise Hays to align my positive mindset with the rest of me. I understood that my journey required patience, rejuvenation, and rest, but sometimes, all of my required components were mentally sickening. You see, I could be extremely patient, and it was clear that I had been, but there were days when I felt tired and annoyed by all the consistency and the footwork, I was putting in. There I stood, working 90 to 100 hours a week to keep my household organized and my children on track, make enough time for my family, and squeeze in a three-hour nap if lucky. I did all this consistently while practicing the art of being a good person with integrity. Meanwhile, the results were still slow, skewed, or invisible to my overwhelmed human eye. As you can imagine, I felt pissed off with my process and wondered who it was. God thought I was. Since I was a child, it had always been drilled in my head that "the lord doesn't put anything on you that you can't handle," yet there I stood, trying to figure out if God himself had made a mistake and accidentally taken me for wonder woman instead of the tired, overworked, overwhelmed dreamer I was on most days. Why did he think I was so strong? Had he not observed the burnout I felt internally and externally occasionally? Had he not witnessed the level of discipline and consistency I secreted doubtfully? Due to these components, I often had periods where I tried to understand why my proving my strength often led to me having to continuously prove my strength and patience, which was often draining. After diving into countless periods of contradictory thoughts, I stumbled upon the teachings of Neville Goddard and Abram Hicks, and my thought process started to shift over time. There is so much creative, inspirational content in the world, and often, it's hard to know what to take and leave. But something about listening to Abram and Neville made me feel like I had been guided to their ideologies by a higher power. I remember the first day I came across Abram Hicks's content video and listened to her speak. Instantly, the words that flowed out of her mouth religiously began to resonate with my soul as I felt a frequency vibrate over my entire body as I took in the video. I thought about the many topics she touched on and would listen to the ones that resonated the most redundantly. I listened as she touched on releasing past shame and guilt, believing in yourself, and mastering your vibration to transform your life. I remember thinking to myself where has this content been? I remember thinking about what changes I could have made early on in my life had I had access to her philosophies much sooner. Although that was my thought process, I understood that things find you at the perfect time. Listening to Neville Goddard, I started to understand the law of attraction more, and I was formally introduced to the law of assumption, which I found extremely interesting. I started to break down the ideology of the law of attraction, which led me to the epiphany that changed my entire complex around the idea. I soon learned that the law of attraction does not send you what you want based on what you desire; it sends you what you want based on who you are. This led me to understand that I misinterpreted the concept of manifesting altogether. Instead of wishing for the vision, I needed to become the vision. Feel the vision, embrace it, and most importantly, call it into my now, owning it in the current space I was operating in. This helped me to clear my head of all the self-doubt that had plagued me during moments of discontentment, poor traction, and mental strain due to putting in the work and dreading the slow results. When I thought about the process of being and the law of assumption, it made sense to me how being the thing and feeling as if it has already arrived could be a pivotal step in acquiring what you seek. I started doing daily exercise every morning when starting my day, where I would find a nice, quiet, calm place to sit and meditate for ten to fifteen minutes. Afterward, I would do a visualization exercise to envision myself in a space where I had everything I was working towards. I would sit in silence, allowing the vision to expand while picturing what my goals looked and felt like in a way that was all currently taking place. I did this multiple times daily, allowing myself to feel less anxiety and anticipation for my visions while transforming them into reality. It's amazing how life can be so chaotic, yet all it takes on our behalf to see a shift is a change in how we think, act, and feel. It was as if the drama, trauma, and chaos I had previously known had disappeared suddenly. I was no longer utilizing my thoughts to keep me trapped in the past, shame myself with guilt, or feel victimized by my experiences. I could feel the internal shift taking place and see how the shift in my inner world affected my outer world. The past no longer plagued me, and I was moving forward in a way that felt good but was never anticipated. It's funny how when we go through the tides of life, we can never see a good outcome, no matter how much we desire. So many times, I wanted a better existence, but I never knew what that would look like for me or if it was something attainable given all that had occurred in my life. Seeing myself in this new space where I looked good, felt good, and learned how to be patient and appreciate my process while I manifested multiple dreams and goals felt good. It was as if I had finally hit the reset button successfully, and God was sending me resources along the way to help keep me motivated, inspired, and humble as he continuously transformed me into the person I had always wanted to become. I had days where I was terrified of the results I was seeing, simply because I couldn't believe how far God had brought me internally after all of the trials and lessons. Healing from so many hardships can be challenging but it felt good to witness the strength God had poured into my heart. I had never had it easy, but I had also never been afraid of a fight. Most days it seemed like fighting was all I knew how to do, and that my friends is a flex within itself. I was no longer bitter from the hardships I had been dealt because I could now see the blessing in every lesson I had been forced to learn. Life has a way of showing us ugly truths daily that we most times aren't ready to face. Life had forced me to take a long hard look at the people in my life, myself, my behavior, and the behaviors of the people around me. I started to understand how things had gone the way they had and why and I was in a new mental state where I no longer felt the heavy weight of self-doubt plaguing me as often as it had. I soon realized the more I thought, felt, envisioned, and spoke positivity over my life the more positive results I fostered. Had I been a culprit in my own past failures? Had I allowed self-doubt to take over me to the point there was nothing festering in my existence but fear and anxiety? The answers were yes and yes, I had. Like many I had experienced things that robbed me of my confidence and joy many times but instead of fighting those experiences and continuing to show up for myself I caved in and allowed the loud whispers of fear to impede upon my essence dragging me into a deep pitch of uncertainty. I remember the day I decided to trust my gut and allow God to take the lead instead of leaning on my own understanding. The spiritual powers of the universe can be strong and abrupt, but they are even more powerful when you learn to trust what God is telling you to do verses what the ego conveys to you. I had always been a person who believed in playing it safe, but I realized no real progress could be fostered out of fear and stalling crossing the threshold towards the purpose God had planted on my being. I had always been someone who was practical and believed in the power of preparation. But is there ever any real way to be 100% prepared for the day? Although I often tried to be ready for anything I soon realized it was not logical simply because life has a way of showing up in an unexpected form ready to rob you of the what if's you anticipated by delivering the what if's you never saw coming. I started understanding the power of faith and what it will do in your life. So many times, I had relied on building my faith around the things my eyes could see. Never taking into account that the real magic happens when there is nothing visible to the human eye. I sat in the chair at my clients' house working overtime in my mind as I began to fathom how it was, I had walked into so much increase all within a twenty-four-hour period. The day before I had spent my time working around the clock , went home to my kids, did laundry, cleaned up, made sure everything was in order for my kids, and spent what time I could with them before laying down to close my eyes for the allotted three hour nap I was used to taking before having to get up and exit the door again to go work doubles at the facility. I had been doing this along with running my business and juggling nonstop for a long period and I was starting to feel the sting of burnout. Day after day I would juggle, give up a shift here and there when I could to get more rest, or spend time with my kids. Yet there was this longing inside my heart that was tugging at me saying "we are tired"! Although I knew I was tired I still felt like I had a long way to go before I would start seeing the increases in abundance, I needed in order to live a more balanced life. Next thing you knew one-day I woke up and everything had arrived.

CHAPTER 14

Time Flies When You're Single Mothering

*B*eing busy and juggling can be hard, but the upside is that you are so busy trying to make traction that your days pass faster. I started to see that the more I took on, the faster my time clock went, which was always good. Except for the days I had off when I noticed my naps were cut short because the five-hour nap I desperately needed felt like a two-hour nap. As soon as I lay down in my bed, it felt like five seconds later, the clock had fast forwarded and boom …it was time to get back up, shower, get dressed, and go back to work. Although the passing of time can have its pros and cons, there was one con I was not prepared for, and that was watching time swallow up my children and spit them back into the world as older, wiser teens who would soon be ready to leave the nest and head off to college. My children had always been my center and one of the biggest blessings in my life. Often, I would glance at them and feel a level of love and unconditional peace when I viewed them making developmental progress that at one time was a challenge due to their experiences. My son was now a teenager, and despite the events due to his father's absence, he was growing into a great young man. As a mother, I had always tried to do my best, recognizing that although that was the case as a woman, I could never teach my son how to be a man, but what I could do was teach him how to be a good person. Instilling qualities of love, compassion, and wisdom in him early on. While also allowing him to rely on my brothers as his muses for what a good man encompasses. I wish I could say that raising kids was as open and shut-off a process as I had hoped, but it had never been easy. But unlike the many challenges I had faced, motherhood was the one challenge that gave me unwavering purpose, and my children were my best friends. I hadn't been fortunate like many around me to have genuine, long-lasting relationships with people, and I found that I preferred the solace of staying to myself most times. I found that although I could be around people for long periods, engage, and enjoy the company of others from time to time, it was not something I preferred consistently. My son had started stepping up to the plate, helping with his little sister, and helping out around the house a lot more after hearing me complain numerous times about how his main focus was spending his day glued behind a computer screen or video game console. The Irony is that Darius in the Diary of Janay Wilkerson had been named after my son, and I had created most, if not all, of the character's personality after my son. My youngest had been diagnosed with anxiety and had been having a rough time at school, so I felt it was essential that we all stepped up as a family to pour into her as much as we could to try and help her push past her anxious flooded events and learn how to cope. Sure enough, we all stepped up to assist her, which was a hard battle no matter how we approached it. She had days where she made lots of progress, while I couldn't even encourage her enough to go to school, watching as she suffered from anxiety attacks and utilized avoidance mechanisms to get through the day. After trying numerous approaches, I got her to start riding the school bus again and going to school every day, and that progress alone felt like a win because it was hard getting her to that place. Shortly after, I started seeing a shift in her; she would come home excited about her school day, sharing stories about her new interactions. It felt good to hear because I knew how hard it had been for her, and we all watched her go through the anxiousness. As a mother, we often need to be able to pause, take a break, and welcome in the peace we are deserving of. Unfortunately, for many of us, that isn't the case because no matter what we are dealing with, we have to master the art of putting those things aside and putting the needs of our children first to promote healthy development, which can be challenging. Being a mother and a serial juggler is not easy, and although I may have made it look easy, I knew it was only because of God that I could navigate motherhood the way I had. I feel blessed anytime I observe my will, way, and discipline toward the matter. My kids could say I was a workaholic, a chronic yeller who dabbled in dropping the f-bomb anytime I got tired and felt like they were not respecting my calm approach. A bossy routine-based entity who loved doing the same things repeatedly, never growing tired of a good old-fashioned routine. But they would never be able to say that I was not a good mom simply because I woke up every day taking pride in being their only trusted resource and companion. Despite their ability to always show it, I knew they were all thankful for me and the life I provided them with. My cursing like a sailor could appear to be an understandable vice for all I carried daily. My oldest had been setting goals for herself and crushing them before my eyes, making me proud to watch her follow suit. For years, my daughter had struggled with her weight, and it caused her many issues both internally and externally. After hearing the urgency in her voice when she came to me, expressing that she was ready to be disciplined and make real changes, I reached out to UVA Children's Fitness Clinic to start the process for her. This turned out to be one of the best things for her, and six months after being consistent with exercise, portion control, and meal prepping, she was at a healthy size, flourishing internally, and gaining confidence in the areas where she previously hadn't had much, and slaying like the fashion girl she always wanted to be but felt she couldn't because of her weight. It's amazing how we can get so caught up in the future that we fail to take notice of all the beautiful blessings in our present space. I had been in grind mode since 2015, working my butt off in so many areas, and during those days, I was terrible at showing gratitude for my current life because I was too focused on building my future life. But I learned that gratitude is one of the biggest components of abundance. So, I made it a habit to look at my now and give thanks, and watching my children thrive made this an easier task to remember. I remembered the days when my oldest daughter and I would sit and talk about her weight loss goals, and we would scour the internet window shopping for looks she would like to wear once she lost weight. As soon as the weight started falling off, we would go to Target, consistently filling baskets with clothing and accessories for her. Afterward we shared ideas about looks we could put together. Before she lost weight, shopping had always been a horrible experience for her. We would go to the store, and I would watch her become unattached to the event while my other two children threw anything and everything into the basket they desired; she, on the other hand, would show no interest. And sometimes, it would make her sad. Each time, it would break my heart because despite her ability to see, she had always been drop-dead gorgeous with or without the weight, but I knew that was something she had to come to realize on her own, and no matter how much I told her she would only see when she was ready to see. Suddenly, it was as if you couldn't tell her anything because she could now see what I had witnessed. After dropping the weight and going to school dressed like she was ready to rip the runway daily, I started to see how she had opened another can of worms I wasn't ready for. That can of worms consisted of hormonal teenage boys who were now flocking around her as if she was a piece of fresh meat, and that pissed me off because I knew there was nothing I could do to stop that attention from coming her way. As horrible as it is to admit, there were so many days where I dreaded the weight loss and glow-up she now displayed due to the multiple hate flooded events she was now experiencing from girls who never saw her coming and the crazy boys who didn't have boundaries and didn't understand their raging hormones. Days like those were when I wished she had not prospered as fast as she had because, as it turned out, I was so unprepared to deal with all of that. But I made do with my uncomfortable emotions, kept our lines of communication open as always, and instilled the proper morale so she would remain humble, make sound choices, and not become so overwhelmed by those opposed to her progress. There we sat once again as mother and daughter going through similar experiences and relying on the love and empowerment from one another to get through it. Moments like those made me realize that although I had not been lucky enough to find a friend group of women who responded to me properly or gave me the love and encouragement I gave freely, I was fortunate enough to get that from my daughter, who had always been noticeably wise and mature for her age. This was when I would take moments to thank God and show gratitude for my now because it is so easy to call God out for the future, he has not provided to you yet. Still, it's noble to call on him and thank him for everything you already are and have. I was starting to recognize that who I was and where I was now was a monumental blessing that deserved to be recognized and honored daily. Simply because I knew where and what I had come from, and getting to where I currently was internally and externally had not been easy. Prom weekend came, and let me just tell you, I have never been as stuck in thought, memories, and tears as I was that weekend. As I watched my daughter smile, twirl, and laugh, looking like she had stepped out of an old Hollywood magazine with her classy satin dress, beautiful textured full afro garnished with butterflies, and a face card that never declined a day in her life due to her radiant beauty that was one of the first things I noticed the day we first met. There she stood in our kitchen, prancing around at age seventeen, ready for her first prom, and all I could think about was that at that age, I was also attending prom, young, misguided, scared, and pregnant with her. Afraid of what the future would hold for me and my unborn child, I sat in my kitchen seventeen years later, looking at the first beautiful creation I had ever manifested. Taking notice of how, although she had been cultivated from poor choices, lack of esteem, and an unhealthy environment, she was perfect in every way I could have ever hoped she'd be. There she stood, twirling in her dress, drenched in the armor of the wisdom of her ancestors, heightened intellect that could not be ignored, a strong, powerful voice that was drenched in the armor of feminism, activism, and compassion, and a radiant, beautiful, glow that was the same radiant energy I was first acquainted with all those years ago as I witnessed her wave to me in the ultrasound that ultimately saved her from an aborted fate. I looked at the fact that I knew at that moment what I had known on the first day I learned of her existence: that she was and would be destined for a life that was and is filled with purpose. Everything I had ever been that was right and of God was instilled in that child, and I could say with an unwavering level of pride that she was all of me and then some. And that had been the goal since day one. I would have never imagined that coming from what I did, I could have the ability to raise children in the way I had, and there were so many days I was afraid of their outcome because I believed a woman on her own could not have such progress. I am grateful that I was wrong. Who would have known that all those years of struggles, fear, independence, and hardship could be transformed into the young girl I was viewing, filled with everything I had hoped she would be? People often say time flies when you're having fun, and although that is true, they fail to acknowledge that time flies for many reasons. Time flies when you juggle like a crazy person, building a future that requires strain and sacrifices, consistency, and, most importantly, time flies when raising kids. Although I could anticipate that fact, it didn't stop me from yearning for a moment or two when I could stop the clock or simply slow it down and hold onto my babies a little bit longer before releasing them into the world of young adulthood and lessons, I knew were essential for their development.

CHAPTER 15

Freaky Friday

My daughter Kylie had just entered her senior year, and I was happy to see all the progressive changes she had made over the summer. After she had voiced that she was ready to change her health, I connected her with the fitness clinic, helped her change her eating habits, encouraged her to adapt to meal prepping and cooking, and encouraged her to develop a workout routine that was easy to follow. After a few months, she started to shed weight, and it was easy to assess all the physical and mental changes she was enduring. I was happy for her and mostly proud because I had witnessed firsthand how intense her journey had been, but I knew several people would not celebrate her glow-up. She started to witness how the friends that had always been her friends were starting to treat her differently, and it was hard for me to watch simply because I felt triggered by her experience. I remember the days of being the underdog and having people in my circle encourage me, not because they believed in me or wanted better for me, but simply because, in their minds, they never thought I could achieve better. It saddened me that when I analyzed my daughter's situation, her experience mirrored mine. It's easy to tell the overweight girl she can lose weight when you've never been overweight; you don't think she is confident, capable, or diligent enough to do so. But what do you say to the girl who shows up over 100 pounds thinner, glowing with confidence, heightened intellect, and a newly developed sense of self that does not allow her to receive the crumbs life was spoon-feeding her before? As I pulled up to the bus stop on the first day of school, I looked over at Kylie and could see the look of anxiety plastered all over her face. "Mom, I'm nervous; what if everyone stares at me," she asked as her mind started diving deeper and deeper into the what ifs of high school life. "If they stare, let them, shit what Megan say…. "I ain't never ask to be the it girl. don't call me sis cause I'm not your sister," I said as I quoted Meg the stallion religiously, trying to lighten the mood and make Kylie laugh. I realized right away my joke was not giving what it was supposed to give. Usually, I could spark a laugh or two from her, but that morning, she was a million miles away, and I could tell from the daunting expression on her face. It was during that moment that I came to understand how perplexed she was starting to feel. It was apparent that losing weight and achieving her health goals was just as complex for her as when those goals were a million miles away from her grasp. I watched as she stepped out of the car, gaining the attention of a long-term friend and former coworker whose lips hit the floor as soon as she witnessed her full image. I could tell this kind of response made Kylie even more uncomfortable. But I watched as she smiled, held her head high, and tried to continue with her morning. Weeks passed, and I watched as she spent most of her days locked into the same routine that had brought her progress. She would wake up and get dressed for school, becoming increasingly accustomed to the fashion girl-centered attire she had always wanted to wear, eat a healthy breakfast, prepare a healthy lunch, then return home after school, and walk for an hour or two everyday no matter what went on. I was overwhelmed with joy to see her finally stepping into the person she always wanted to be, but it was also beautiful to see her grow and understand herself properly. Simply because this was an area she struggled in previously. It is easy as a parent to tell our children how awesome they are, especially when we have the privilege of seeing firsthand the beauty they encompass. But it is a hard ass assignment to get them to truly see themselves and all the possibilities hovering over their lives. So much of my existence had always been wrapped up in my children and at times throughout my motherhood journey I questioned if I could help them in the ways I knew they desired for me to the most. It is a challenging task being a one woman show and prior to my children becoming teenagers I had worn the role of the single mother as if it were a badge of honor. I was now starting to have different feelings regarding the matter. Sure, it was a blessing to be able to handle the role and responsibilities on my own, but I was no longer welcoming the thought process that was formulated around me being alone in all my responsibilities. I wasn't in a rush to change that dynamic, but I was now welcoming the idea of trying to find "my person." The person who would come into my life and make things easier, love and protect my children as if they were his, support me in my endeavors without an envious response, and provide for me in the ways I felt I deserved and desired.

CHAPTER 16

Babes in Budget Land

W hen I first set out to write these stories, my initial goal was to inspire women and men to leave toxic relationships. Having seen numerous abusive interactions during my thirty-five years of living, I realized how common those connections were. It also became apparent to me the types of people on the opposing end of the abuse spectrum. Whether you are dishing out the abuse or the person receiving it, the act is toxic and destructive for both parties. After sharing my trials in Baltimore Imprint, I realized that the cycle of abuse doesn't simply flee from your side after you have left the situation. The battle you were fighting physically may have ended because now you no longer have to live your days waiting for the moment you will find yourself in the ring with your opponent, exchanging blows verbally and physically. But what do you do to repair the components of your life that have been hardened by your experiences, such as your mental health, your financial well-being, or your connections with others that have become distant due to you straining away the good relationships in your life while you try to hold onto the toxic one that is currently draining the life from you day after day? After removing myself from all of the poor relationships in my life, I started to see how, despite my traction, there was still much work left to do regarding my behavior patterns, coping mechanisms, and plan for growth. So many new changes were happening in my life, but there was still a long list of changes I was trying to execute daily. I started clearing my path of all the negative, fake, envious, selfish, untrustworthy, and so on. This process, which started to be complicated initially, became fairly easy for me once I realized that my holding onto relationships with those types of people showed a lack of esteem. Once you understand who you are and what you deserve, you sit in a space where you vow never to allow certain experiences again. This is when you know you have grown and are in an authentic space where real healing has occurred. I had allowed people to abuse my mind, heart, body, finances, and time while being in these poor one-dimensional relationships. I realized I needed to rejuvenate all of those areas of my life. You can't get back money spent and time wasted or repair your wounds overnight. What can be done when you have previously suffered these sorts of fates is you can rebuild from the ground up, placing boundaries in the areas where there were none, being disciplined, and valuing yourself in a way that allows others to interpret what can and can't be done about your being. I decided the best way to tackle these issues would be to place myself on a life budget. I would budget several components of my life to enhance things and get things back to a place of homeostasis and happiness. The first thing I tackled about my life budget was people. Although we tend to highlight that people don't matter, in the grand scheme of things, they do so often. This statement is hypocritical when you take the time to dive deeper into other people's components and their impact on your life. People can sprinkle gems of positivity or negativity into your life. This causes you to respond in numerous ways, sometimes leading to unbeneficial behaviors, dissections, and thoughts that all ultimately limit you and hinder your process. One of the ways I tackled this issue was by learning to reprogram my thoughts and behaviors, which was hard as fuck. Initially, I found it hard to shut off thoughts brewing since the beginning of time. I also found that, most times, it's easier to produce a negative thought versus a positive one. I realized that if I had nipped the issue long before it cultivated into a thing, I would have had more success handling other people. I started learning to be quieter in spaces where I was first acquainted with others or knew I would only be temporary. Some might argue that being quiet or silent is a form of dimming your light in a sense, but I had learned that no matter what I did or didn't do, my light could not be depreciated, and that was sometimes more of a curse than a gift in my experience. I was no longer allowing people to be in the know about me if they didn't already have that information. I tried showing up as "no one," disclosing only what was necessary and leaving out the majority of the facts I used to share innocently in the past that would cause others to want to hinder me. No more sharing who I was, what I was doing or going to do, or what I believed in. I decided that information was privileged, and moving forward, I would only share in safe spaces where sharing was permissible and done amongst people who were like me or more progressive than me. People who wouldn't know my essence, goals, or lifestyle feel away. This was a great change, and I admit I still had unfavorable experiences where people would feel triggered by me or show envious behaviors. Still, the number of experiences died down significantly. I decided to take this further after noticing that my social media views had started shooting through the roof. The likes were nonexistent, and the support was wishy-washy, but the views would increase weekly, making it clear that the small town I lived in was still operating as a small town. Making it clear to me that there were a lot of extra eyes on me that shouldn't have been in most cases. I decided that as much as I loved sharing my journey via social media, documenting by utilizing video and photo imagery, it was time to take a much-needed hiatus from social media. I had done this many times, but something was nudging me, inspiring me to do it on a more disciplined scale. Whenever I considered the matter, six would stick out in my mind. So I decided the best thing to do would be to pull away for six months and get my brain focused in a way I hadn't been for a long time. Social media can be a great resource, especially for those with aspirations and entrepreneurial endeavors, but I have never had a real following on social media. The majority of my followers consisted of a bunch of small minds from a small town who were not in support of my journey, couldn't believe how much traction I had made, and would have rather jumped off a bridge than support me, but were all too invested in deleting me. So, the views were consistent day after day, and the numbers grew, but the interaction and support did not. I realized I had wasted much time, posts, and energy on social media, and instead, I could redirect that time and pour it into my craft, research, education, and family time. I started looking at this matter from a scientific perspective, viewing it as the perfect experiment opportunity. I thought about the time it took to create an image, create the proper caption with hashtags, post, and monitor the traction of the post, views, and response. What would my life look like if I decided to remove my social media engagement time and utilize it for other things in my life that I knew would be progressive and could not be presented as a waste of my time? After sitting with my thoughts and analyzing them properly, I knew choosing to be out of sight and out of mind regarding social media would be a great opportunity. It would also depreciate the evil eyes distributed towards me and my endeavors from those obsessed with watching and waiting for me to fail due to their disdain for me and my evolutionary process, which was not one they had anticipated being real or last. Unfortunately, for some, social media constantly triggered them as they tuned in to find that I was still favored, protected, and progressive despite their hopes for me to be otherwise. After placing a six-month budget on my social media time, I moved on to my actual budget to see what changes could be made to enhance my credit, spending, and savings. Bookkeeping had never been a fun task, in my opinion, but I knew I would have to start being a little more structured in my recordings of everything that went out, came in, and stayed in if I wanted to get my capital structured properly. I decided the best way to do this was to track my multiple income sources weekly and monthly. After documenting everything I had coming in for the month, I started recording all the monthly amounts that were extracted from that income due to bills, credit repair, food, kids, and unexpected expenses. After tracking what came in and what went out, I set a realistic budget for myself of what could be spent and what could be saved per month while including my monthly bill responsibilities and tuition goals. As you can imagine, when I plugged in the numbers and considered my three kids, groceries, tuition, bills, and topping that off with a side of inflation, my eyes were stressed and strained, but I knew it could be done, and it had to be if I wanted to get to the next level in my life. After starting these two areas, I still needed to address two life budgeting areas: self-care and family, which were the two most important on the list. Yet, due to the restraints of goals, grinding, and being my only resource, these two things often felt like they never received enough attention, and that was something I wanted to change permanently. I worked two full-time jobs after my business slowed down and transitioned away from its six-figure status. I had been fortunate enough to make more as a caregiver than ever while advancing in the field, but I also saw how that sometimes came with uncertainty due to death and illness. Although it was difficult when a case ended, I never allowed myself time to stress about it because I knew that was also a part of the business. I also knew it didn't take much to find a job while I waited for things to pick up. I had worked as an overnight supervisor while working cases during the day, then as an insurance agent, and taken cases with other agencies while I continued to drift along the entrepreneurship roller coaster ride. I had left numerous jobs during that period that were overwhelming or simply just not a good fit with my schedule and lifestyle, reminding myself not to be afraid of the changes going on all around me because, like always, God would cover me and get me to where I needed to be and that was something he always delivered in my direction no matter what. I also left jobs with great income, but I knew the time constraints were not a good fit for the things I needed to do for my kids, education, and goals. Each time I did that, I would question if I had somehow become delusional and lost my mind while recognizing that healthy doses of delusional were helpful while on my journey. I had never closed a door and not witnessed a better one open instantly, so I knew everything would work out in time. Although I was the queen of hustle and grind, I was starting to feel differently about things. I had always been a person who did frequent self-assessments, and during my assessment periods, I would ask myself things that I knew needed to be answered to make the best choices regarding my path forward. One of the questions I knew I needed answered was Nina, how does the hustle make you feel? When looking at the question, my answers came to me quickly. I felt stronger, empowered, willing, able, diligent, committed, and most importantly, tired. Sure, I could do it that way, but why did I have to? What would happen to my path and outcome if I decided to do things differently? What would happen to my mind and body if I honored it with more sleep and rest periods? This is when I decided to be less of the queen of taking on overtime and more of the queen of self-care. Let me just say that this was hard as fuck, and it was mainly because, over the years, I had cultivated an addiction to work, which some might argue was a healthier addiction to have, but it was not. I also realized it had been cultivated out of the fear of failing, falling, and missing my mark. This, my friends, is a common fear for a single mother, but it should not have been for me. This was a major disservice because I had seen God's deliverance when I was less faithful and less committed, and diligence and ambition were completely absent. How could I ever consider that the Nina who was now self-aware, diligent, structured, and committed could lose if the Nina who had never been those things hadn't lost? A door had never been shut off to me without a better door showing itself, and based on the knowledge of that, I reconsidered my stance and said fuck it, let's get some rest! My days off were my days off, and that was how I kept it. I was not lifting a finger to do anything constructive unless it was laundry that couldn't wait, errands for my kids, or writing because when a story comes, you have to grab it and see where it takes you, and that was always my mechanism! I started seeing how my new life budget was helping me to get to where I needed to be mentally and physically. It had always been apparent that my mind and body could endure much more than the average human, but just because it could didn't mean it should. After landing there, I decided it should remain a place to sit while I continued pushing forward, trying to reach my parenting, educational, and entrepreneurial goals. Growth is often met with challenges; in my experience, those challenges can be more bewildering than they should be. But something we have to consider is why that is the case. How can we ever truly grow if we are unwilling to allow the universe to stretch us in uncomfortable ways? Challenges offer us insight into who we are and who we have the potential to become. As I have shared with you all through my texts, you have come to know the many faces of struggles and triumphs I have had the privilege of knowing. While I can admit that I have not always been optimistic when presented with change, I have come to understand how the tides are always working for us, even when it is apparent that we don't feel that way during the initial process. The more the tides of life feel like they are working against us, the more I know that this is when God is rewriting our story to move us to a better space. One which we never see coming. I had never been one to live life on a budget, and before making certain changes, I always considered a budget in the financial sense and not the spiritual, mental, or physical sense. I established my life budget to set boundaries for others and myself. Increase my financial, mental, and physical well-being. And increase healthier behavior patterns that promote the abundance I have always searched for. Although the tides of life have never been predictable, making certain changes can help them to be less overwhelming to our process. I hope that by sharing my transparent account of the tides of my life and the changes I have accustomed to, I will inspire someone else to welcome necessary changes and do the work to grow and reach their full potential. Life will never be perfect, and there is no human on the planet who is without flaws, but there is a way for life to be perfect when paired against imperfection. Transitions are challenging and usually unwelcome, but they are the window into our next. They should be met with optimism, preparation, and commitment if we truly find that our goal is to elevate and enhance our lives in all the areas we can. As I continue on this long-term journey of growth, abundance, and self-discovery, I find that the path is always made clear but not always easy to follow. With that being the case, I am grateful God blessed me with the discipline I now have to be steadfast and persevere despite the obstacles that have arisen along the way. I hope that my sharing my stories and allowing a front-row seat to my manifestation journey will inspire others to know that change is possible and that you can overcome anything, no matter how lost you may feel in the healing process. Nothing happens overnight, and even though we live in a world where instant gratification is glamorized, televised, and falsely distributed as a real option, I hope my readers will understand that nothing in this life that is worth having comes to you instantly. Hard work, commitment, discipline, and understanding always have to propel you toward your dreams and goals for them to manifest and become permanently established. With that being so, the waves of change should be welcomed along your journey because these waves are an essential part of the process. So, I advise you to learn to ride the waves until they allow you to drift to your final destination. I hope you all will join me again soon for more stories and insight as I continue my journey of being, becoming, and sharing, allowing the imprints of my experiences to imprint the life of another!

CHAPTER 17

The Tides of Change

She stood hovering over the water, glimpsing her still reflection, wondering what it was about all the change that made her feel numb. Had she not seen this before? And if she had, was the memory so far from her now that she somehow could no longer sense the feelings in real-time? She glanced at the water again, remembering the days that had passed. Thinking, remembering, and thanking the universe for the relief she had come to know. With every tumultuous memory, she watched as the still water became lively, roaring in the distance. She watched the tides become unhinged, rolling in the background, calming each time she professed gratitude for the outcomes she did not properly anticipate. She stared deeper into the water, watching as her image became clearer as she assessed her now, compared to the days she had known before that were more chaotic. What was this new feeling she had now grasped as the irony of the past began to slip away? Had she finally found a peace that could be hers? Her mind began to dive in and out. It was pulling her back and forth as she fostered up the dysfunctional memories of the past. Memories filled with pain, shock, betrayal, and disappointment. She began to allow all the discomfort to flourish as she took an elongated glimpse at the past. She had sat with these memories and experiences for far too long. Sure, they were a part of her, but for how long? Was she destined to carry these painful imprints with her for all her days? Or could she now allow the tides of life to wash them away as she dreamed of the day, she could peacefully own new experiences that did not leave her bare in the ways she disliked? She began to focus on one memory at a time. She was allowing herself to relive the experience as if it were yesterday, and she was still embedded in the scornful events. She relived each imprint before silently tossing the memory into the roaring tides, watching as the water engulfed her pain, sweeping it away as if it had never existed. She stood at the water's edge, still gazing at her image, taking heed to the moon's reflection as it shimmered in its full status, shining on the bed of water that now held all the days of her past. She watched as the stars appeared in the night sky, taking over her interest. As she began to count them all, noticing that there was now a star shimmering for each unfortunate event, she had turned over to the tides. She felt an essence soaring inside her, clearing her spirit of the past's ugliness. She filled her lungs with new air that was of a fresher quality than the air she had breathed before. She felt her heart begin to beat synchronously, beating more calmly. As she took notice of the tachycardia leaving her body, she was rejuvenated in the ways she had always hoped. There no longer was any sight of doubt, disrespect, disappointment, betrayal, humiliation, or heartbreak. She watched as the tides returned blessings to her for each imprint she had willingly distributed into the water. Allowing each discomfort to sink to the bottom, resting on the water floor, never to be seen again. She watched as her reflection began to rise from the water in human form, reaching for her hand. She delivered her hand without delay, allowing her reflection to take her in its arms. She began to relax as she felt the reflection wrap her in its arms as it pulled her downward into the water, taking her under for a few seconds before bringing her back up and disappearing afterward. She felt renewed as the baptism cleansed her loins, leaving her imprinted by the spirit of a higher power that had given her the internal components she had desired for some time. The tides had indeed changed, washing away the mildew-encrusted past and presenting a present full of growth and change.

www.ingramcontent.com/pod-product-compliance
Lightning Source LLC
Chambersburg PA
CBHW030311130626
46549CB00002B/811